WOW!
Resumes for
Financial Careers

Other titles in the WOW! Resumes Series include:

Chuck Cochran and Donna Peerce, *WOW! Resumes for Sales & Marketing Careers*

Matt DeLuca, *WOW! Resumes for Creative Careers*

Rachel Lefkowitz, *WOW! Resumes for Administrative Careers*

WOW!
Resumes for
Financial Careers

Leslie Hamilton

McGraw-Hill

New York   San Francisco   Washington, D.C.   Auckland   Bogotá
Caracas   Lisbon   London   Madrid   Mexico City   Milan
Montreal   New Delhi   San Juan   Singapore
Sydney   Tokyo   Toronto

Library of Congress Cataloging-in-Publication Data

Hamilton, Leslie
    WOW! resumes for financial careers / Leslie Hamilton.
        p.   cm.
    Includes index.
    ISBN 0-07-025563-6
    1. Résumés (Employment) 2. Financial services industry--
Vocational guidance.   I. Title.
HF5383.H25   1998
808'.06665—dc21   98-11881
                                                                CIP

McGraw-Hill

A Division of The McGraw·Hill Companies

    2 3 4 5 6 7 8 9 0 MAL/MAL 9 0 3 2 1 0 9 8

ISBN 0-07-025563-6

*The sponsoring editor for this book was Betsy Brown, the assistant
editor was Kurt Nelson, the editing supervisor was Fred Dahl, and the
production supervisor was Pamela Pelton. It was set in Stone Serif by
Inkwell Publishing Services.*

Printed and bound by Malloy Lithographics, Inc.

Contents

5 Resumes That Use Unconventional Formats—How to Build a Resume That Looks Truly Distinctive   **49**

6 Resumes That Take a Bold Graphic Approach— Jazz Things Up Visually   **75**

7 Resumes That Quietly Overcome Obstacles— Emphasize Your Strong Suits   107

8 Resumes That Take Big Risks—Practical Tips When "Desperate Times Call for Desperate Measures"   143

9 Don't Send It Off Yet!—Double-Check Everything   161

Alphabetical Listing of Resumes

Preface

Objective: Develop a resume that stands out from the pack, stops readers cold, and gets hiring officials excited about the prospect of learning more about you. That can at first seem a daunting task, but rest assured that writing a superior resume is a skill you can develop with a little practice. Helping you build up that ability—with minimal damage to your psyche—is what this book is all about.

Here you will find dozens of models of finance resumes that emphasize positives, make compelling cases for their writers, and show exactly how to win positive interest. Also included are strategies for developing the right customized resume for you … and, I hope, plenty of inspiration for you as you set about the task of building a resume that gets you the interview and the attention you deserve.

Whatever level of employment your financial job search is targeting, you'll find, within these covers, the tools and resume models you need to get the reaction you want to hear from prospective employers: Wow!

About the Author

Leslie Hamilton (Boston, MA) is an author and researcher who has written and contributed to many books on careers and personal finance. Her other books include *The Cheapskate's Guide to Living Cheaper* and *Sound Smarter Than You Are*.

1

The Finance Hiring Game

What Top Hiring Officials Want to See—and What They Don't

In creating, the only hard thing's to begin; a grass-blade's no easier to make than an oak.
JAMES RUSSELL LOWELL

Sometimes, simply following the rules is the worst way to go.

Take the task of finding a job within the field of finance. While following what we perceive to be established procedure may make the most sense when it comes to fulfilling the responsibilities of certain finance-based jobs, it's not necessarily the best way to get the attention of a hiring official. Like just about everyone else these days, the people who make decisions about whether to hire you are pretty busy. They need more than a factual recitation. They need to hear about realistic potential solutions to the difficult problems they face every day.

Peter F. Drucker recently wrote on this topic in the *Wall Street Journal* (March 29, 1995). Drucker's remarks are worth reviewing closely here:

"Most resumes I get ... list the jobs the person has held," Drucker wrote. "A few then describe the job that the person would like to get. Very few even mention what the person has done well and can do well. Even fewer state what a future employer can and should expect from that person. Very, very few, in other words, yet look upon themselves as a 'product' that must be marketed."

KEY POINT

As a practical matter, you *shouldn't* expect a resume that obediently lists every position you've ever held, and does little else, to get superior results for you.

What Drucker is calling for, I believe, is a completely different type of resume than the ones many of us are accustomed to writing or reading. We're looking for a resume that will make hiring officials break their routine and say, "Hey, wait a minute!"—or better yet, "WOW!"

The objective, then, is to formulate a WOW resume. This is a resume that takes responsibility not simply for listing job titles, but also for supplying information about "what the person has done well and can do well." Some people will tell you that finance is an inherently conservative field and that resumes for financial professionals must, as a result, avoid the marketing-centered approaches Drucker's remarks point toward. I disagree.

Aggressively highlighting possible solutions to the problems decision makers face on a daily basis is, in my view, the only intelligent approach to resume development in today's employment market. What follows is some practical advice on developing a WOW resume, and examples you can use as you craft your own.

What Decision Makers Want to See

An informal canvassing of insiders familiar with financial hiring decisions at companies large and small resulted in the following "what they're looking for" categories among prospective employers:

Strong core knowledge of basic financial principles and accounting

The ability to apply those principles to a wide variety of situations

A working knowledge of the financial and economic environment in which the hiring company must operate

Strong verbal and written communication skills

General familiarity with the world of computerized information management (although experience in specific software environments is not always essential)

Your resume will stand or fall on its ability to dramatically broadcast your capacity for achievement in these and related areas. You can make your resume command attention through creative use of a number of basic elements, including: a heading with pertinent contact information; a "grabber" introductory section (typically either a professional summary or a targeted objective of direct interest to a particular employer); an extensive employment section outlining responsibilities, skills, and accomplishments; and a brief overview of your educational qualifications.

In addition, you may wish to add a separate category at or near the end of your resume, one I'll call the "Hey, look me over" element. Traditionally, this part of the resume has carried headings like Other or Personal, with the unfortunate result that applicants have used this section to talk about their fondness for checkers or the names of their pets. Striking and directly relevant material should show up in the "Hey, look me over" section—information or insights that define you as a person and a potential employee. You may decide not to use this final element. However, notice in the sample resumes how the final portion of your resume offers you a great chance to set yourself apart from other candidates—and that's the name of the game.

Chapter Two presents an in-depth discussion of the core purposes of your resume.

Creative Pestering

KEY POINT

The applicant who finds the most creative, persistent ways to pester is usually the one who gets the offer.

Before we move on, let me leave you with another important piece of job search advice. Taking responsibility for the job search itself makes all the difference. I call the most effective method of taking responsibility—rather than ceding it to, say, the personnel department—*creative pestering.*

Pester? Is that really the word we want to use? Well, yes, but there is a caveat. By pester, I don't mean be a pest, but rather continually find ways to get yourself onto people's to-do lists in the nicest possible way.

Creative pestering *doesn't* mean...

* Leaving indignant or annoying messages on voicemail systems

* Adapting a superior attitude with receptionists and administrative support staff

* Appearing combative or adversarial during the interview

* Pulling crazy stunts that are likely to get you thrown out of the joint (like the overbearing applicant who decided to camp out in the president's office until the Top Banana agreed to a personal meeting)

* Wearing down key decision makers by declaring some kind of personal vendetta against the target company

Creative pestering *does* mean...

* Doing the research necessary to make valuable proposals and suggestions—for free—that benefit the hiring official
* Following every apparent "no" with a question about future hiring patterns, and staying in touch with decision makers who've turned you down to ask about new hiring initiatives
* Proposing intelligent part-time contract assignments on your own initiative
* Offering to buy decision makers an early breakfast to get the latest information on hiring within the company or industry
* Making countless pleasant phone calls (the "pleasant" part is vitally important) in order to develop or learn more about professional opportunities

The model resumes that appear in this book will serve to forward your candidacy in a dramatic way. When combined with a strategy of creative, persistent pestering, they will help you land that great job you deserve.

2

Some Resume Basics

What the Resume Is Meant to Do

The greatest truths are the simplest.
J.C. AND A.W. HARE

The reason most resumes don't fall into the WOW category is simple. Most people who write resumes have serious misconceptions about what, exactly, a resume is meant to do. What is the purpose of this ubiquitous document? What's it meant to accomplish? What are one's objectives in writing one? What *shouldn't* one expect a resume to do? Once you resolve these questions, you'll be in a much better position to craft a resume that makes decision makers stop and say, "WOW!"

What a Resume Isn't

A resume is not an application for a position.

Prepare yourself for a shock: The vast majority of resumes are completely ignored. In fact, so many resumes are sent blind to decision makers that the act of popping one in the mail, and doing nothing beforehand or afterward, amounts to little more than an exercise in wishful thinking. The bubble-bursting reality is: *Putting your resume into the mail does not, in and of itself, represent a meaningful form of outreach to a potential employer.* In fact, a fair number of experienced career counselors warn strongly that one's resume should never be mailed, period. Instead, they counsel, sending a superior letter (like the models that appear in Chapter 3) and eventually telephoning is a better initial form of outreach for making new contacts.

KEY POINT

No matter what you may read or hear to the contrary from the prospective employer, you shouldn't think of yourself as having applied for a job if you haven't talked to someone within the company about it. For most employment settings, the don't-mail-the-resume advice is solid. You're far better off putting together a punchy written appeal that makes your cold call to a decision maker at a target company just a little warmer, or calling existing members of your own network and developing new contacts and leads in that way. To paraphrase the Beatles, mailing out resumes without making any personal contact is a bit like trying to get a tan by standing in the English rain.

Once you've established some kind of relationship with the contact at your target company, then you can make arrangements for an in-person meeting, formal or informal. That's the time to pass along a version of your resume that makes sense for the opening in question. A well-structured letter, like the ones that appear in this book, can help you overcome the send-in-your-resume-and-then-we'll-talk trap so familiar to people who make job-related networking calls. All the same, I recognize that the temptation to send a resume and see what happens can be incredibly strong. Because there are a few (and I do mean very few) situations when you may be forced to send a blind resume and cover letter, you'll want to take a look at the discussion of these situations that appears in Chapter 3.

A resume is not a single document you can write once and consider "finished."

Please *don't* make the (time-consuming) mistake of believing that a job search consists of developing a single resume, finding advertised openings, and mailing out copies of your resume until something happens. Instead, get on the phone with friends and associates, send out letters to new prospective employers (see Chapter 3), and target each resume you send out. By doing so, you'll set yourself apart from the pack. It's certainly true that not many people actually like writing resumes. Most people want to write a resume once and mail it to 50 different employers. That probably explains why these documents so rarely have any direct bearing on the employment openings they're supposed to help applicants track down.

The resume you pass along to a decision maker should be focused specifically on the company or position in question. A fair number of the sample resumes in this book model the perfectly reasonable and entirely accurate step of listing as an Objective the specific job at that company that the job seeker is pursuing. This is a much sounder course of action than stating your objective from your own perspective (e.g., "Locate a position within a dynamic firm that will allow me to grow professionally.") You should be ready to use your computer to customize not only a single line, but all essential elements of your resume's text. *Learn what problems the decision maker is hoping to resolve, and then focus your resume on those problems!*

A resume is not an affidavit.

It's an advertisement, a marketing tool, a device that must include every (accurate!) statement it possibly can to forward your candidacy.

Many job applicants, and particularly those seeking finance-related positions, make the mistake of slavishly following preestablished formats or patterns to pass along the "right" information. The right information is that which inspires the decision maker to pursue your candidacy further. Any sample resume you encounter, including those that appear in this book, should be considered a *suggested* format for adaptation to the specific situation you face.

What a Resume Is

A resume is meant to be scanned.

Long, dense blocks of type have a way of turning hiring officials off, although there are certain situations in which they can serve you well by amplifying points specifically raised by the prospective employer earlier in the process.

Most (though not all) of the resumes that appear in this book feature condensed "talking points" rather than long essays on particular aspects of one's work experience. There's a reason for taking this approach: *Virtually no one reads resumes*, at least not in the early stages of your contact with the target company. Expect your resume to be scanned quickly, not studied minutely.

A resume is a convenience for the hiring official.

Shocking news! The resume is really a way to screen you *out* of the organization. That's right—the decision maker typically uses your resume to make more or less instantaneous

KEY POINT

You may have only a few seconds—perhaps a few *fractions* of a second—to make or reinforce a positive impression with the resume you create.

"yes-or-no" determinations about your candidacy and the candidacies of literally hundreds of other applicants. There's almost always a big pile of resumes from potential applicants. The hiring official has to make that pile disappear, and thus almost always uses resumes to find out who *doesn't* match the requirements. That saves the time that would otherwise have to be devoted to countless face-to-face discussions with eager applicants.

Make sure your grabber introductory material really does grab! Since people tend to zip to the bottom of the page, make sure that the "Hey, look me over" text you select to close out your resume reinforces the message, "This one looks interesting." Within the body of the resume, isolate benefits and make the reader curious about finding out more in a hurry! Speaking of curiosity...

A resume is an opportunity for you to leave the reader wanting to learn more.

Insofar as the resume serves as a silent spokesperson in your absence it must, like any good advertisement, eventually inspire your audience to action. In most cases the outcome you're after is a simple one: You want the person to pick up the telephone and either offer you the job or ask you to come in and discuss the job in detail. The objective is not to supply a full-blown professional biography, but to supply enough telling facts for the reader to make a decision to contact you.

After all, you'll want to save some of the heroics for your face-to-face discussion with your contact!

Now that you've gotten a good idea of what your resume is supposed to do, you're ready for...

Twenty Big Questions That Will Help You Develop Your WOW Resume

Here are twenty questions to ask yourself about your own work history and education. Schedule a time when you can devote at least 90 uninterrupted minutes to the development of written answers to each of these questions. That's five to seven minutes per question.

Jot your answers down in a looseleaf notebook. Give your best-guess answers for now. Be honest, and don't let yourself get bogged down in technical details. If you find yourself thinking that answering a question fully requires some in-depth research on your part, leave that aspect of the question blank for now and make a note to come back to it later. For now, get down the broad outlines of your answers to each of the Big Twenty.

1. What are the three most dramatic examples of verbal or written praise you've ever received from any supervisor or client? What awards, commendations, or formal acknowledgments have you received in any work setting?

2. What was the most recent job you held? (If you're presently employed, this will be your current job.) List the most important duties.

3. What skills do you/did you have to develop to deliver superior results on the job in that environment?

4. Think of at least three situations when failing to do something you do/did in that work environment would have resulted in disaster for your employer. How much money, time, or resources would have been required to rectify the problem?

5. Think of at least three times a supervisor in this position outlined a problem for you to solve—a problem you *did* solve successfully. What was the positive outcome of each of those solutions? Did you make a system or procedure run more smoothly? If so, how much more smoothly? Did you save money? If so, how much money? Did you save time? If so, how much time?

6. Think of at least three instances when you personally saved the day as part of your work on this job, perhaps by thinking quickly in an emergency or acting responsibly during trying circumstances. Did a computer ever crash, leaving you to pick up the pieces? Was a customer ever angry over something you were able to resolve? Was a deadline ever moved up to a date that seemed impossible, but wasn't?

7. Answer question 2 for your next most recent job.

8. Answer question 3 for that job.

9. Answer question 4 for that job.

10. Answer question 5 for that job.

11. Answer question 6 for that job.

12. Answer question 2 for the job you held before that.

13. Answer question 3 for that job.

14. Answer question 4 for that job.

15. Answer question 5 for that job.

16. Answer question 6 for that job.

17. Write down the specifics of at least five situations when coworkers came to you for help and you were able to provide it. What was the worst-case scenario that was averted by your taking action? What positive outcome emerged instead?

18. Make a list of any extracurricular activities you may have pursued in school that provided you with experience that either directly related to the finance position you'd like to win or required you to develop significant leadership skills.

19. Make a list of any charitable activities that directly relate to the finance position you'd like to win.

20. Make a list of at least 15 people—former employers, colleagues, professional associates—who would be willing to develop short written recommendations for you or would agree to endorse a recommendation you composed.

As you peruse the resumes in this book, you'll find that most of them make use of the kind of information this questionnaire asks you to develop. By taking time now and devoting a good, solid 90 minutes to answering these questions in writing, you'll put yourself in a position to highlight what employers really want to see: potential answers to pressing problems!

In the resume you develop using the models that appear in this book, you'll be able to provide the potential answers to those pressing problems in the form of...

Compelling (legitimate!) endorsements from third parties

Examples of performance that saved time or money or increased efficiency

Instances when you took the initiative and forestalled disaster

Those are the kinds of elements that make up WOW resumes. There are dozens of examples of these types of items in the pages that follow. Take the time now to develop the material that puts you in the best possible light.

There Are References and There Are References

Some resume-writing authorities take a dim view of attaching written references to your resume on separate sheets of paper. I have to agree that this tactic looks a little desperate, and it's all too easy for the separate endorsements to become separated from your resume. (My experience is that a good many managers resent anything that adds to the clutter factor on their crowded desks.) That's not the same thing, however, as incorporating the highlights of written or spoken endorsements in the body of your resume, which can be a very powerful tool indeed.

In Chapter 9, you'll find a couple of brief, helpful checklists—summaries of resume and employment letter commandments, if you will. Those lists will help you evaluate your written appeals and make them as sharp as they can possibly be. For now, take the time to answer the Big Twenty Questions in detail. That work is the foundation of the job you'll undertake later, to develop a superior resume based on the samples in this book.

Please do not continue on to the next portion of this book until you've completed the questionnaire work in this chapter!

Use Resume Models for Job Search Success

There are dozens of examples of superior resumes in this book that will help you to take the raw material you develop by answering the questionnaire and use it to write your own WOW resumes. As you examine the models, be prepared to adapt elements from more than one resume. Use what works. Use what makes sense for your situation.

When You Get Stuck

It happens to the best of us: Sometimes you run dry while you're working on your masterpiece of aggressive employment self-promotion. Don't panic. Find a constructive way to get around your roadblock.

KEY POINT

Adapt the formats of appropriate resumes—whether they follow a chronological format that examines dates of employment, a functional format that emphasizes key skills of interest to a particular reader, or a combination of the two—with an eye toward making a dramatic, confident, positive impression on your reader.

Here are two strategies to consider when you find yourself staring at that long, blank sheet of white paper while setting up your initial notes; or if you've finished your questionnaire and are transferring your work into a more polished form on your personal computer, and that insistent cursor keeps blinking whether or not you've got something interesting to say.

Strategy One

Take a short break. Get up for a minute or two to have a drink of water or pop a high-energy tape or CD into the music system. Most cases of writer's block come when we're pushing ourselves unreasonably, trying to turn out something when our minds have been on the case for too long. As long as you don't use the drink-of-water routine as an excuse to keep your stretches of constructive work from disintegrating into a four-minutes-on, two-minutes-off charade, you can usually get further by allowing yourself a modest break between (for instance) fifteen- to twenty-minute time slots spent working on your resume. When you hit a wall, find a way to clear your mind. Don't just keep demanding new results from the same exhausted brain cells. Also effective, and worthy of consideration if you've just taken a short break: Move on to another section of your resume, and come back to the problem section that has you stumped a little later on.

Strategy Two

Use a Superstar Verb for inspiration. The most powerful parts of your resume will probably be sentences that begin with active, results-oriented verbs. ("Maintained 99.85% error-free contact database for use by sales force.") Here's a list of over 130 action verbs. Play a little game with yourself and write ten sentences that describe your own work background, each of which begins with a verb that addresses the area that's got you stuck.

Superstar Verb List

Accepted (responsibility, heavy workload challenge, etc.)	Accomplished
Acted to	Acted as troubleshooter for
Adapted	Adjusted
Administered	Advised
Allocated	Analyzed
Appraised	Approved
Arranged	Assembled
Assigned	Audited
Authored	Authorized
Balanced	Briefed
Budgeted	Built
Calculated	Catalogued
Chose	Clarified
Compiled	Computed
Coached	Conducted
Consolidated	Convinced
Coordinated	Critiqued
Customized	Cut
Decreased	Demonstrated
Designed	Determined
Developed	Devised
Diagnosed	Directed
Dispatched	Drafted
Edited	Eliminated
Established	Estimated
Evaluated	Executed
Explained	Facilitated
Forecasted	Formulated
Found	Founded
Headed up	Hired
Identified	Implemented
Improved	Increased
Informed	Initiated
Inspected	Installed

Instituted	Instructed
Interpreted	Interviewed
Invented	Launched
Learned	Lectured
Led	Limited
Managed	Marketed
Monitored	Motivated
Negotiated	Operated
Organized	Originated
Overhauled	Oversaw
Planned	Predicted
Prepared	Prioritized
Produced	Programmed
Promoted	Prospected
Publicized	Published
Qualified	Reached
Reached out	Recommended
Reconciled	Recorded
Recruited	Redesigned
Researched	Resolved
Reviewed	Revitalized
Rewrote	Saved
Scheduled	Screened
Selected	Set
Shaped	Showed
Simulated	Sold
Solidified	Solved
Specified	Spoke
Strategized	Streamlined
Strengthened	Summarized
Supervised	Surveyed
Systematized	Toured
Trained	Trimmed
Turned around	Upgraded
Wrote	

3

The Supporting Cast
The Lowdown on Letters

Invention breeds invention.
RALPH WALDO EMERSON

Many people are surprised to learn that the look and feel of one's written job search material can have a surprisingly powerful impact on the final decision maker. Rest assured—it's true!

I strongly suggest that you coordinate your written job search correspondence by picking a particular, striking set of stationery and sticking to it throughout your correspondence with target companies. The paper you choose doesn't have to be expensive or visually overwhelming (in fact, it probably shouldn't be either), but it should broadcast professionalism in a consistent, understated way.

When the time comes to make a final decision about a new hire, the odds are good that your contact within the organization will make a final review of the written correspondence received from all applicants. How much do you think it will aid your cause with that decision maker to see that your resume and the series of letters accompanying it all share the same tasteful color scheme and basic look? This may seem a small consideration, but believe me, paper selection can make a difference. (So can the decision to type or word process all your letters if your handwriting isn't exactly the world's neatest.)

I've already mentioned the dangers of mailing your resume. Let's examine this point in greater depth now as it relates to the alternative we'll be discussing in this chapter—pre-resume letters.

There are three main points to bear in mind when it comes to popping your resume into the mail. They are:

1. Secretaries and administrative assistants routinely screen out unsolicited resumes. As a general rule, they're paid to do so! That means that no matter what you say in the cover letter, there's a very good chance that someone other than your intended recipient is going to spot the resume and put your correspondence aside for "later review." Think about how often *you* get to the business correspondence you set aside for later review. That's about how often hiring officials will make the time to scan your resume.

2. Secretaries and administrative assistants virtually never know the difference between a resume someone has asked to see and a resume that's been sent cold. They may spot your "as requested" notation; then again, they may not.

3. Secretaries and administrative assistants *don't* screen most personalized business-related correspondence. That is to say, if your correspondence does not include a resume, it stands a much better chance of making it through to its intended recipient, especially when you're contacting employers about something other than advertised openings.

What does this all add up to? *Mailing resumes blind is, statistically speaking, more likely than not to be a waste of time, effort, and money.* On the other hand, sending a broadcast letter—a dressed-up letter that offers more pertinent detail about your career than an untargeted letter might, but less than a resume would—is likely to mean that a decision maker actually sees what you've written.

Are there some situations in which you'll be well advised to send a resume and a top-notch cover letter? Sure. The hiring official may be located in another city, and may demand to see a resume before asking you to fly out to discuss an opening. The hiring official may have lost the original copy of your resume that you delivered in person. The hiring official may have asked you to develop a new version of your resume and may simply refuse to meet with you personally until he or she has had the opportunity to review it.

All of these possibilities exist, and in these cases you'll need to assemble a superior cover letter, one similar in impact to the samples that follow. But in most situations, your best course of action will be to make virtually any excuse that allows you to *speak* to your contact before delivering your resume in person. The resume you hand over should be targeted *directly* to the needs, requirements, and specifications of the employer with whom you've spoken.

One more important word of advice: Think twice before you get overly creative when it comes to establishing the means of connection between your contact person and your resume or letter. This will no doubt be familiar advice by now, but it bears repeating. Try your level best to find some way to hand the package over yourself, during a face-to-face meeting. That strategy will be far more effective than coming up with an elaborate delivery system designed to get the decision maker to pay close attention to your resume.

Overnight delivery services, bicycle couriers, flowers, gifts, oversized boxes, registered mail—seasoned hiring officials have seen them all, and they're more likely to wonder what you're trying to compensate for than they are to be impressed by your ingenuity. Take the money you were going to spend on renting a marching band or a small jet plane and put it back into your bank account. Set aside another hour or two to make sure the material that's on your resume tells a dramatic, confident story—and does so in a way that's immediately accessible to the reader.

KEY POINT

If you do opt to send a resume through the mail, *never* send one without a sharp-looking cover letter on matching stationery.

The "Perfect" Letter

How do you use written materials to pave the way for a relationship with a contact within your target industry? Here's the single best tool I know of. It shows that you've done your research and that you're willing to take responsibility for cheerleading your own candidacy through the organization. It should be no surprise to you by now that I advocate sending this letter *without* a resume and following up by phone; however, the model letter can also serve as a superior cover letter on those rare occasions when you need to mail a resume. Just add the sentence, "My resume is enclosed" to the beginning of the paragraph before "Yours truly."

Date

John Miller
ABC Corporation
456 Main Street
Mytown, State 00000

Dear Mr. Miller:

Jane Owens, in your Human Resources department, tells me that you're looking for a Senior Widget Inventory Manager Specialist.

ABC's Requirements	*Jane Smith's Experience*
College degree	Bachelor's degree in Accounting from Worcester University, 1984
2 years experience with Widget Manager inventory control software	6 years of experience with Widget Manager inventory control software
4 years experience in a widget industry environment	6 years experience in a widget industry environment with American Widget
Knowledge of widget industry fulfillment patterns	Knowledge of widget industry fulfillment patterns
Familiarity with basic spreadsheet applications	6 years experience with spreadsheet programs including Excel and Lotus 1-2-3

I think we should talk about the ways I could make a significant contribution to ABC Corporation. I look forward to speaking with you soon.

Yours truly,

Jane Smith
123 Main Street
Mytown, State 00000

(617) 555-1212

P.S.: I will plan on calling you at 9:00 a.m. on Tuesday, July 16th. If this is not a convenient time, please give Robin a better time for me to reach you.

This simple letter—which requires, as you've no doubt noticed, that you do a little phone research to determine the nature of the open position and the name of the receptionist, secretary, or administrative assistant—is the single most effective weapon in your arsenal when it comes to making contact with decision makers. That's not to say that it's guaranteed to get you an enthusiastic return call. No letter will always do that. But it *is* virtually certain to capture the interest and attention of anyone who reviews the mail, say, once a week and has a vague appreciation of the fact that his or her organization is looking to hire a widget inventory specialist.

When you follow up by phone as promised, you're likely to hear a thoughtful pause and the rustle of paper as your contact searches for that intriguing letter that crossed the desk a few days back. That's what you want to hear. When your contact fishes the document out of the pile, find an opportunity to ask repeatedly and politely for an in-person meeting to discuss the position. If time allows, ask the person what he or she is trying to get accomplished in the area you're interested in. Odds are you'll get some meaningful feedback—and some inspiration on the best way to target your resume for the meeting.

The beauty of the two-column approach is that you *only focus on matches between what you offer and what the prospective employer wants.* You don't bore the reader with your life story, and you don't supply lots of details that don't fit into the "right profile" the hiring official is responsible for tracking down. But what if you don't have any idea about the requirements of the position? Suppose you're doing all the right things—avoiding fixation on the classifieds, isolating fast-growing employers, devoting a certain period of the day to make cold calls to managers—and you don't know whether there's an opening that's right for you at a promising company. You can still use a letter to your advantage. Consider the two samples that follow, each of which can, like the one you just saw, be adapted to those infrequent situations when you must pop a resume into the mail.

Date

John Miller
ABC Corporation
456 Main Street
Mytown, State 00000

Dear Mr. Miller:

According to *Business Week*, the American widget industry is poised for "significant expansion into Eastern European and South American markets" within the next two years (*Business Week*, January 16, 1998, page 123). I applaud the groundbreaking work your firm is doing to expand into these new markets, and would love to be able to help contribute to your firm's steady growth.

I gather from the *Business Week* article that your company is among those attempting to significantly increase business in these areas of the world. That being the case, you're likely to need help managing increased levels of inventory. I offer you:

> 5 years of superior high-efficiency performance in a widget inventory management environment

> Superior computer skills and deep knowledge of both WidgetManager and Lotus 1-2-3
>
> A team-first attitude and the ability to work both independently and as part of a workgroup

I will be in your area next week. I would like to visit with you so we can discuss how we might be able to work together to increase efficiency and reduce inventory management costs at your company.

Sincerely,

Jane Smith
123 Main Street
Mytown, State 00000
617/555-1212

P.S.: I will plan on calling you at 9:00 a.m. on Tuesday, July 16th. If this is not a convenient time, please give Robin a better time for me to reach you.

By the way, my experience is that the P.S. is the very best place to serve notice as to what you plan to do next. The more you're able to customize the P.S.—for instance, by making reference to a secretary or assistant—the better off you'll be. If you reach that secretary or assistant, don't get haughty or start ordering him or her around. Treat this person exactly as though he or she were the Big Boss.

Here's another example of an eye-catching cover letter that paves the way for a personal phone call. This one does the trick by highlighting a single example of superior performance that leaves the reader wanting to know more.

Date

John Miller
ABC Corporation
456 Main Street
Mytown, State 00000

Dear Mr. Miller:

I was named Inventory Manager of the Year at my company's national awards dinner last year because I reduced stockouts by 64% after only six months on the job.

I'm a computer-savvy, goal-oriented team player who follows the widget industry closely. The January 16 issue of *Business Week* leads me to believe that expansion is in your company's future, and that you'll soon be in need of a qualified inventory specialist like me.

Let's meet to discuss the possibilities!

Sincerely,

Jane Smith
123 Main Street
Mytown, State 00000
617/555-1212

P.S.: I will plan on calling you at 9:00 a.m. on Tuesday, July 16th. If this is not a convenient time, please give Robin a better time for me to reach you.

As you've probably already gathered, I'm a big believer in the "less is more" principle when it comes to job search letters. (I think the same basic principle applies to resumes, by the way; I've met too many hiring officials who hate reading multi-page resumes to feel otherwise.) The aim, after all, is not to drown the (probably overloaded) reader in new facts, but to elicit that simple WOW reaction that leads naturally to the question, "When can you come by for an interview?" I've talked to many hiring officials who felt overwhelmed by a resume that left little to the imagination … and often, little to discuss with the applicant.

Here's one more effective employment letter that you may use as a model, one that's based on a previous phone conversation between you and your contact. Note how it takes the bull by the horns—that is, takes responsibility for a dramatic next step—and how it employs effective appeals based on points raised during your call.

Date

John Miller
ABC Corporation
456 Main Street
Mytown, State 00000

Dear Mr. Miller:

It was great to talk to you recently concerning employment opportunities at ABC. I was particularly intrigued by what you had to say about the new widget outsourcing program, which I understand needs to be up and running very soon. With your permission, I'd like to put together an outline of an agreement that would allow me to help ABC develop a detailed plan of attack for your project on an independent contractor basis, including recommending vendors and developing training materials for the new software you'd need.

I'll plan on faxing my outline of how we might be able to work together to your attention this coming Friday, and I'll follow up by phone the following Monday.

Thanks for taking time to speak with me!

Sincerely,

Jane Smith
123 Main Street
Mytown, State 00000
617/555-1212

P.S.: I will plan on calling you at 9:00 a.m. on Monday, July 15th. If this is not a convenient time, please give Robin a better time for me to reach you.

Talk about creative pestering! The letter above provides an excellent example of exactly what that looks like when it's committed to paper. Did your contact volunteer anything about your working as an independent contractor for ABC? No, but there's certainly no reason not to bring the subject up yourself, especially if you've got some insight about where the company is going in the near future. Did your contact say anything about talking to you on Monday morning about your outline? No, but simply faxing the material would probably lead to a long silence. What's the harm in following up persistently and politely?

Now it's time to take a look at the stars of our show—the model documents that will help you craft your own WOW resume! As you make your way through the resumes, remember that you're going to be talking to more than one potential employer over the course of your job search. That means you'll need more than one resume. Don't wed yourself to a single model from the examples that follow. Pick the format that provides the best fit with your situation and then customize it to the needs and interests of the person and organization you're targeting.

4

Resumes That Use Daring Headlines

How to Start Your Resume with a Bang

To have begun well is to have done half the task.
HORACE

A hundred and fifty other applicants at your target firm will be using familiar, and boring, lines to launch their resumes. A couple will even have committed the classic mistake of labeling the resume with the self-evident phrase, "Resume." Not you. In this chapter, you'll find model resumes that use the opening line to powerful and dramatic advantage.

ACCOUNTING MANAGER

A strong lead-in to a compelling summary of high points. Note the careful selection of key points designed to capture the interest of a single, targeted employer.

John Smith
123 Main Street
Mytown, State 00000
111/000-0000

A WORLD OF EXPERIENCE!

Education

Chartered Accountant (CPA equivalent. Bachelor of Commerce, Morocco National University, 1988. Emphasis on Banking, Accountancy, Commerce, and Marketing.)

Experience

Bank of Morocco, Marrakech, Morocco / Accounting, Systems and Compliance Dept.
July 1992 to present

As a manager in the Accounting, Systems and Compliance Department, my responsibilities include:

* Global consolidation of accounts and preparation of the Group's financial statements with an accounting team comprising 5 staff who report to me.

* Personal responsibility for drafting the Group's annual financial statements in accordance with International Accounting Standards and prevailing practices.

* Compilation and submission of all statutory returns to the Moroccan Monetary Agency [Central Bank of Morocco].

* Ongoing support for branches, subsidiaries, and representative offices in over 20 countries.

Taylor International, Marrakech, Morocco / Senior Accountant
November 1989 to June 1993

As a senior accountant with Taylor International, my experience included:

* Analyzing problems and proposing solutions for clients in a wide variety of industries, including insurance, manufacturing, banking, and construction.

* Monitoring the success of peer assignments.

* Training junior staff.

* Reviewing written training materials for regional training workshops.

* Developing a special policy manual on the detection of embezzlement of funds. This manual was later distributed companywide and was credited with the identification of over $200 million in fraudulent transactions.

The dramatic use of the third person highlights this applicant's ability to develop new software skills quickly. An excellent example of a resume for someone in a mid-level position who wants to enhance his or her upward mobility.

John Smith

Is An Experienced Financial Professional Who Knows How to Deliver Results in...

Financial Accounting
Cost Accounting Analysis
Design of Information Systems Organization
Finance Control

(What's more, he's skilled in Lotus 1-2-3, Word, and Peachtree, and can get up to speed quickly in virtually any other program that has to do with delivering superior performance in an accounting environment.)

Northeastern New Zealand Accounting Guild, Auckland, New Zealand * Member, June 1995 * Major in Accounting (Industry and Commerce) * Minors in Cost Accounting, Business Administration, and Finance Controlling.

B.S. Degree, Accounting, University of Chesapeake Bay, 1992

Experience

Commerce Central
New York, NY (June 1994-June 1995)

Accounts Specialist
Responsible for bank reconciliation and all credit card transactions. Prepared monthly foreign exchange reports to government agencies. * Prepared daily bank balances report to chief accountant. * Maintained manual ledger accounts and cash book for McKee Restaurants International.

Mann World Industries
New York, NY (March 1993-June 1994)

Assistant Sales and Marketing Manager
Helped to set and review sales and marketing targets. * Developed creditor age analysis reports; arranged credit terms and periods. * Represented the company at an important seminar (Chicago, Illinois) on marketing and management of exports to West European markets. * Developed formal recommendations for senior management that led to highly successful international export program.

123 Main Street
Mytown, State 00000
111/000-0000

If this headline doesn't capture the hiring manager's attention, he or she is probably in a coma. Some variation on this line may well be appropriate to your situation.

Jane Smith
123 Main St.
Mytown, State 00000
111/000-0000

Professional Highlights

In just eight months, took First Savings of Pennsylvania's Commercial Loan Department's defaulted loan rate from thirty-sixth out of thirty-six companywide (highest percentage of bad debt in the company) to fourth place. **That year, I was cited as "One to Watch" in a major industry trade magazine.**

Personally responsible for on-site coordination of a mainframe database system for Real Estate Owned properties (First Savings of Pennsylvania). **The organization had previously tracked all properties via a paper filing system and several unlinked PC databases.**

Served as a voting member of the Loan Review Committee (Pittsburgh Trust). **Selected after only six months on the job.**

Managed a commercial real estate portfolio of $34,000,000 (Pittsburgh Trust). **The youngest manager ever assigned this portfolio.**

Assisted Regional Manager in sale of institutional properties by using my special knowledge of Assisted Real Estate property budget creation and case presentation; property valuation; coordination of management, leasing, and marketing efforts; establishing appropriate sales prices; data compilation and analysis of real estate holdings; income/expense operating analysis; appraisal review and critique; and commercial loan workout strategies (Pittsburgh Trust). **Our efforts set a regional sales record.**

Supervised Processing, Closing, and Marketing Departments while assuming full responsibility for auditing loan files for accuracy and compliance (United Financial Corporation). Awarded **"Woman of Many Talents" plaque at annual company dinner.**

EMPLOYMENT HISTORY

Asset Manager/Financial Analyst
Pittsburgh Trust
June 1995-present

Assistant Financial/Credit Manager
Pittsburgh Trust
July 1994-June 1995

Loan Originator
United Financial Corporation
January 1993-July 1994

Assistant Financial/Credit Analyst
First Savings of Pennsylvania
January 1992-January 1993

Sales Associate
Hentworth Clothing Stores
January 1990-December 1991
(This part-time job paid most of my college expenses.)

I have a bachelor's degree in Business Administration from Tidewater University (Miami, Florida). I graduated 14th in a class of 347.

COLLECTIONS REPRESENTATIVE

John Smith
123 Main Street
Mytown, State 00000
111/000-0000

COMMITTED TO INCREASING YOUR PROFITABILITY!

Seeking a challenging and fast-paced collections position that will take advantage of my significant interpersonal skills and proven personal initiative to **reduce your bad debt.**

"John Smith knows how to make cash flow numbers look better in a hurry."
—Jane Stephens, former supervisor.

1/95 - 8/97

Senior Collections Executive, American OverCell Phone Central, Chicago, IL

General office duties; set up cellular phone accounts; **reduced uncollectable debt by 14% in a three-month period.**

Named **employee of the month** for January, 1995.

Worked with sales reps to insure **minimal loss of goodwill** among current customer base.

Brought significant **bonding and negotiation skills from** past assignment to new role as collections agent.

12/93 - 12/94

Sales Representative
Cell Phone Central, Chicago, IL

Successfully **completed** inaugural training session.

Interacted with current and new customers.

Kept up regular daily calling routine that resulted in **$75,000** worth of new business for the company.

Personally oversaw management of **$350,000 sales territory.**

Education:
Yourtown State College, Associate Degree in Business, 1993

An arresting opening line helps to overcome any perceived mismatch, given the applicant's background in nonprofit organizations. The resume is targeted toward a specific financial analyst opening in a for-profit environment.

Jane Smith
123 Main St.
Mytown, State 00000
111/000-0000

SOLUTIONS FOR HIRE: I offer five years of hands-on bottom-line experience in a challenging, fast-paced financial management environment.

Work Experience

Pennsylvania Library Network
Institutional Finance Manager
November 1995 to Present

As the senior finance officer I have:

* conducted financial analyses of member Pennsylvania public libraries
* made funding recommendations to the Pennsylvania State Library Science Commission and Pennsylvania Legislature
* developed institutional publications summarizing financial data for member organizations
* provided critical support for junior-level finance officers in accessing and developing computer database systems
* provided essential user support of internally developed programs
* offered interpretation of finance-related laws as they pertain to member organizations

I was praised for "consistent, reliable oversight of our financial operations" by the outgoing Director of our organization, Frank Velez.

Institutional Finance Officer
November 1993 to November 1995

I was responsible for:

* overseeing and fact-checking publications of financial data
* supporting changes in computer database design and manipulation
* conducting audits of submitted financial information from member organizations and establishing consistent guidelines for the submission of revisions and updates

I was the youngest Institutional Finance Officer on the staff for my entire period in this position; in November, 1995, I became the youngest Institutional Finance Manager in the history of the organization.

Intern
August 1993 to October 1993

Handled data entry and general office duties on a volunteer basis.

At the conclusion of my internship, I was asked to join the staff on a full-time basis.

I have deep experience in using Lotus 1-2-3, Windows and Windows 95, and Microsoft Office, as well as such Internet-related programs as Netscape. I am familiar with Macintosh environments, as well.

Education

Bachelor's Degree in Business Administration, Wellfleet College, Wellfleet, MA.

I can be contacted by the overland mail at the address above or via the Internet at janesmith@friendnet.com

A winning, upbeat, and thoroughly appropriate headline leads off this resume—and effectively highlights the applicant's international experience.

John Smith
123 Main Street
Mytown, State 00000
111/000-0000

SPANNING THE GLOBE FOR FINANCIAL SOLUTIONS!

My bilingual and analytical skills make me a potential candidate for effectively serving the needs of your company as a Financial Analyst or Market Analyst.

I am …

Experienced in financial and market analysis, and in the development of loan proposals for companies seeking capital

Skilled in International Market Analysis

Proficient in C++, COBOL, and Pascal

Experienced with UNIX, MS-DOS, Windows 95 and OS/2

Fluent in reading, writing and speaking Spanish and French

PERFORMANCE HIGHLIGHTS

CoMeriTan (Paris, France)1991-1997

As a Financial Analyst (1993-1997), I performed financial and market analysis for American companies, and developed loan proposals including business plans and cash flow projections totaling over $1,500,000 in investment capital.

As Technical Coordinator (1992), I maintained appropriate inventory levels and maintained relationships with key subcontractors. I also served as translator for Spanish-speaking clients while visiting our home office.

As Database Administrator (1991), I maintained several very large client databases using ACT! for Windows and prepared timely, accurate cash flow projections using MS Excel.

EDUCATION

I hold a Bachelor's Degree in Business from the University of Southern California.

A powerful headline quote instantly sets this applicant apart from the competition. The opening line both sets forth a personal philosophy and demonstrates a commitment to on-going professional development.

Jane Smith
123 Main St.
Mytown, State 00000
111/000-0000

"Only the *right* knowledge is power." — Mark Waldstein, Management Consultant

Professional Experience
Graham Associates, New York, NY (1995-present)

In my current position as **Network Administrator** for this elite international consulting organization, I develop and administer training for financial applications on Graham's customized database software. This requires an in-depth knowledge of report formats, daily production routines, and system maintenance. I also apply my significant experience in costing analysis and reporting to develop and update reports.

Verigood Foods, New York, NY (1994-1995)

As **Finance Data Coordinator** at the national headquarters of this major food processor, I assisted managers in establishing procedures for companywide monthly billing cycles. I trained new hires in the manipulation of spreadsheets for double entry accounting, and served as Network Administrator for a 73-user Novell system. I developed and administered training in word processing, spreadsheets, custom database work, and many other applications.

As a result of extensive work in **various administrative and support positions** on both a part-time and full-time basis, I have long-standing skills in bookkeeping, accounts receivable and accounts payable. Early on in my career I gained knowledge in developing financial statements (including cash flows), financial forecasting, capital budgeting, and human resource management.

I received a bachelor's degree in Finance from the University of Pensacola (1994). **I paid for my own college education by working at part-time and temporary positions during the day and attending night classes.**

FINANCIAL CONSULTANT

Another example of a powerful quote in the headline. This resume works a dramatic endorsement into the first line of text. In order to determine the attribution, the reader must keep reading into the body of the text!

John Smith
123 Main St.
Mytown, State 00000
111/000-0000

Deliverer of "significant cost savings"

SUMMARY

An experienced Certified Public Accountant with B.S. in Accounting from Siddes University who offers:

* Eight years of comprehensive experience in accounting.

* Superior skills in PC-based software - spreadsheets, databases, graphics, and presentation applications.

* A proven track record in developing and implementing mainframe and PC-based accounting solutions.

WORK EXPERIENCE

GUSTAFSON, INC., high-tech startup company, Smallville, IL (1996-Present)
Financial Consultant
Provided all accounting services to this new manufacturing entity building initial production facilities in Mexico. **Spearheaded development of finance- and inventory-related computer training materials in both Spanish and English.**

HYDE ENVIRONMENTAL SERVICES, INC., Moosup, CT (1992-1996)
Senior Accountant
Developed financial reporting systems through advanced use of mainframe and PC systems for this international environmental consulting firm.

STARKEY CORP., Shreveport, LA (1989-1990)
Controller
Held final responsibility for performance of accounting department for this rapidly growing manufacturer. Responsible for all phases of accounting. Prepared financial statements, budgets, cost analysis, etc. Developed customized billing, payables and cost accounting systems. **Developed insurance costs monitoring system which led to "significant cost savings" over existing methods.** (President's report, July 14, 1990.)

EDUCATION
Bachelor of Science in Accounting - Siddes University (Gresham, PA) 1988. **Graduated summa cum laude.**

Certified Public Accountant (1992).

Sometimes the best headline takes the form of a quote that instantly tells the reader exactly who you are and what you believe. Here's an example of a resume that does that in a memorable way.

Jane Smith
123 Main St.
Mytown, State 00000
111/000-0000

"Information technology should operate in ways
that are of the greatest benefit to people,
not the other way around."
— James Noble

CAREER PROFILE

Highly qualified financial/accounting professional with a commitment to delivering quality financial information management services.

PROFESSIONAL HIGHLIGHTS

DataSmart (Oakland, California)

Financial Software Quality Assurance Analyst, 1995 to present.
Contribute as a member of project teams to determine and assist in following a defined, logical process that results in high-quality financial software products. Our products include: SmartTax 4.0, Account Review, Product Launch, and My Easy Business Analyst. (The last two programs were selected as **"Best Releases of the Year"** in their respective categories by Home Entrepreneur Magazine.)

* Utilize software troubleshooting skills and extensive knowledge of business and accounting procedures to help this top-level company develop high-quality software products.

Independent Consultant (Sacramento, California)

Self-Employed Consultant, 1994-1995
Consulted with firms in the packaging, overnight shipping, and biotechnology industries on accounting issues, business management methods, and information systems problems. **Oversaw implementation of six new information systems, each of which dramatically improved efficiency and increased accuracy of forecasting.**

* Established personal marketing plan; exceeded financial goals during both years of operation.
See client/contact list on reverse side of this page.

Seldes Products, Inc. (Ukiah, California)

Controller, 1989-1994
Managed all accounting functions. Selected, installed, and conducted training for new microcomputer network that increased departmental productivity by 47%.

* Personally responsible for development of training manuals and materials for customized software applications.

Mellingham, George, and Leonine, CPAs (San Francisco, California)

Staff Accountant, 1986-1989
Used tax preparation skills to assist clients. Offered assistance in detail-oriented audits and management advisory engagements. **Cited for "consistent accuracy and attention to detail"** in personnel evaluation.

COMPUTER PROFICIENCY

Spreadsheets
> Lotus 1-2-3, Excel, Quattro Pro

Word Processing
> WordPerfect for Windows and Microsoft Word

Database
> Paradox, dBase III+, R:Base, and Access

Graphics
> Powerpoint and Freelance Graphics

Programming Languages
> Microcomputer-based COBOL compilers and program debugging aids, including Microfocus and CA-Realia

Windows 3.1, NT 4.0, 95, and the related accessory tools.

This aggressively self-confident, one-word headline isn't for all employment settings. It's likely to be most appropriate within a sales environment, as it's used here. The inclusion of sports coaching experience near the end is relevant, given the management nature of the job for which the applicant is applying.

John Smith
123 Main St.
Mytown, State 00000
111/000-0000

OVERACHIEVER

PROFILE: A self-starting investment technologies sales management professional with a proven ability to work effectively with both salespeople and senior management. Offer superior knowledge of investment technology products; strong personal client relationship skills; and straight-ahead, results-oriented sales instincts.

December 1994 to Present
Ordway Investments Technology Corporation, Detroit, MI
Vice President - Head of Sales (Institutional Market)

Personally responsible for development, marketing, and sales of trust accounting software, investment software and investments systems. **Exceeded annual revenue development targets by 13.3%** (1997).

* **Closed** first sale for newly formed Ordway Investments Technology Corporation.

* **Supervised** staff of sixteen.

* **Established and implemented** all sales and marketing strategies.

* **Designed** all marketing programs for regional and national trust conferences.

January 1994 - December 1994
InvesTech, Laramie, WY
Head of Sales - Institutional Market

Oversaw development, marketing, and sales of investment research, investment software, Internet projects, asset allocation and investment systems.

* **Exceeded quota** on institutional sales of $350 million in assets generating $700,000 in revenue and profit of $400,000 annually, beating quota by 175%.

* **Supervised** staff of eleven.

* **Set up plan** for direct solicitation and cultivation of trust institutions, banks, and law firms.

May 1992 - January 1994
Jerek Corporation, Brewster, NY
Institutional Marketing Specialist

Oversaw development, marketing and sales of asset allocation and investment software products and services.

* On assumption of new position, installed face-to-face selling program that **outperformed previous direct-marketing approach by 147% during first year.**

* **Hired, trained, and managed** staff of nine salespeople.

* **Exceeded** 1993 departmental quota by 211%.

1991-1992
McCabe University, Indianapolis, IN
Assistant Baseball Coach

Recruited and coached student athletes.

Additional Information

Attended McCabe University (Indianapolis, IN) on a baseball scholarship.

Graduated with honors from McCabe University, 1991; B.S. in Accounting.

An intriguing example of a resume that overcomes the "Would she relocate?" problem in dramatic fashion. Bear in mind that just a hint of appropriate humor within your resume can go a very long way toward setting you apart from your competitors.

Jane Smith
123 Main Street
Mytown, State 00000
111/000-0000

HAVE SKILLS, WILL TRAVEL

08/95 - 03/97 Bravelle International
Consultant/Buyer

* Negotiated a $14 million wool contract in New Demeria (Southeast Asia) resulting in contribution to organization of $2.2 million.

* Prepared and organized meetings with leading investment banks to create a country investment fund for New Demeria.

* Surveyed Brazilian market for wool (data essential to successful conclusion of negotiations).

09/88 - 08/95 Oressco (Producer and distributor of women's garments)

11/93 - 08/95 Manager with main responsibilities in marketing, administration, and sales

* Personally responsible for key human resources functions, including recruitment, training, promotion, and resource allocations.

* Computerized production planning, bookkeeping and inventory management.

* Managed production planning (including sites in Finland and the Czech Republic).

* Organized consignment inventory strategy for selected retailers.

* Developed successful distribution plans for England, Holland, and Finland.

03/91 - 10/92 Accounting Clerk

* Processed bookkeeping work and management of account receivables. Promoted to manager after less than a year in this position.

Education and Training:

10/90 Southern Polytechnic

Bachelor's degree in Business Administration. Graduated with honors (3.7 GPA).

I have completed formal or self-study programs in Excel, Lotus 1-2-3, WordPerfect, Word, Access, and various Internet applications.

I am willing to relocate domestically or overseas for the right opportunity.

LOAN COORDINATOR

Another excellent example of a dramatic headline that incorporates a credible endorsement from a third party. The use of the exclamation point is justified here—but don't overuse it in the body of the resume, or include two or more in succession anywhere.

Jane Smith
123 Main Street
Mytown, State 00000
111/000-0000

"A ONE-WOMAN PRODUCTIVITY SEMINAR!"
— (*Carson City Bank Newsletter*, January 15, 1997)

Overview

Highly motivated, self-starting banking professional. Superior interpersonal skills; strong customer service orientation.

Experience

The Bank of Carson City
Loan Coordinator, Central Processing Division
1994 - Present

Personally responsible for processing consumer and small business loans. Serve as liaison between home office and branches statewide. Develop weekly work schedules and supervise staff of six.

Aromad Corporation
Accounting Manager
1993 - 1997

Selected, installed and troubleshot new systems database, resulting in significant increases in efficiency departmentwide. Compiled market analysis and evaluated state inspection standards to assure compliance. Accurately managed accounts payable and receivable, including invoicing.

Carson City College
Student Assistance Associate
1993 - 1993

Oversaw residential and work assignments of incoming freshmen and transfer students. Served as liaison between college departments. Provided curriculum evaluation assistance to students and parents; regularly resolved financial aid problems.

Education

1991-1992 Carson City College, Carson City, NV M.S.W., Social Work
1986-1991 Carson City College, B.A., Psychology

An innovative pair of headlines demonstrate above-average likelihood for a good fit with the organization. How many applicants will take the trouble to develop a working familiarity with important phrases such as a company's mission statement?

John Smith
123 Main Street
Mytown, State 00000
111/000-0000

Your company motto: "Service is *our* middle name."

My career philosophy: "Service is *my* middle name."

I have four years of experience in a fast-paced financial environment, with extensive accounts payable work. I am eager to make a contribution to your organization as a Purchasing Agent.

WORK EXPERIENCE:

Sharon & Associates (June 1994-present)
Accounts Payable Auditor

Perform comprehensive audits of accounts payable and purchasing organizations. Conduct interviews with potential clients. Praised by senior partner as **"the kind of employee who makes clients feel good about working with us."**

At Sharon & Associates, I've ...

Won the departmental accuracy award three times.

Helped to develop important new accounts by working with my supervisor in creative ways. **Total value of accounts on which I've worked: $2.5 million.**

Developed a set of skills in purchasing and auditing that make quality service contributions in a Purchasing Agent capacity the logical next step.

EDUCATION:

I received a Bachelor's degree in Economics from Central Michigan University (1994).

This punchy headline serves as a natural lead-in to a compelling personal summary. Note how individual accomplishments are broken down into stand-alone, single-sentence chunks.

Jane Smith
123 Main St.
Mytown, State 00000
111/000-0000

A Savvy,
Results-Oriented
Marketing Professional
for ABC Corporation

SUMMARY

An experienced marketing professional, skilled in the use of information technology. Strong dedication to systems integration and the intelligent use of technology to evaluate and attain critical business objectives.

EXPERIENCE

Eastern Household Products, Newark, NJ

Marketing Analyst
March 1995 to present

Promoted into this position by means of a recommendation (unsolicited) from Senior Vice President of Marketing. Develop and transfer critical market-profile information to senior management; reports are used to oversee the performance of Eastern's sales force.

Highly profitably new product launch (SweepTrain handheld vacuum cleaner) arose from research of emerging consumer trends and subsequent recommendations to senior management.

Oversaw data reporting system development for the Company's home office marketing operations.

Spearheaded campaign to update analysis computing platform; new solutions resulted in **significant increases in efficiency.**

Personally implemented the company's first base of workgroup users; **estimated labor cost savings were 65% or higher for habitual computing tasks.**

Field Accounting Support Specialist
September 1992 to March 1995

Offered support for Eastern's payment-tracking software, **used by over 1400 team members.**

Personally responsible for technical support of 37 of United's 146 districts, **including the six largest districts and the entire Mid-Atlantic region.**

Implemented system changes that improved financial performance, reduced processing delays by over 40%, and gathered previously unobtainable debugging data. **Four offices that had historically required frequent visits from technical support personnel were operating flawlessly.**

SKILLS

Extensive computer experience in both PC and Macintosh-based environments. Specific proficiencies include Novell Netware 3.x, Windows 3.x and 95, MS-DOS, Lotus 1-2-3, Excel, and ACT! — but odds are good that **if it runs on a computer and has something to do with accounting or marketing, I know how to use it.**

EDUCATION

Western University, Santa Clara, CA
Bachelor of Science in Commerce, 1994
Major: Finance; Minor: Marketing

An exceptional resume model for an entry-level applicant. Note the use of the quote in the targeted headline, and the concise but powerful Skills section.

John Smith
123 Main Street
Mytown, State 00000
111/000-0000

"A Superior Team Player"
—and an Asset to ABC, Incorporated!

EDUCATION

Straightford University, Charlotte, NC
* B.S. degree expected May 1998
* Double major in Politics and Economics
* Coursework includes: Corporate Finance, Economics of Underdeveloped Countries, Advanced Macroeconomic and Microeconomic Theory, Statistics, International Trade
* GPA 3.75 on a 4.0 scale. Expected graduation with honors (Magna Cum Laude) and with distinction

Coop University, Littleton, MA
* Courses in International Finance and International Monetary Policy, Summer 1997
* Courses in Logic, Linear Algebra and Differential Equations, Summer 1995

Cashfield College Memphis, TN
* Summer Finance Program for high school graduates, Summer 1994
* Fullerton College, Fresno, California, 1993-1994

EXPERIENCE

Beltway Originals, Washington, DC
Accounting Department Intern for this national clothing distributor (Summer 1997)
Praised as "a superior team player with an eye for accuracy" by supervisor Mel Karsten.
Processed accounts receivable.
Spot-checked data entry work for accuracy.
Assisted in the development of training manuals for new computer procedures.
Gamma Epsilon House, Littleton, MA
Treasurer for this campus fraternity (1994)
Balanced checkbook.
Established purchasing procedures.
Processed check requests.
Developed accurate monthly reports.

SKILLS

* Fluent in English and French
* Familiar with IBM-PC, MAC, SUN and DEC workstations hardware
* DOS, UNIX, MS-Windows, CADD
* Telnet, Netscape, Gopher
* Pascal, FORTRAN

AWARDS

* Dean's List with Distinction 1995, 1996, 1997.

ACTIVITIES

* Straightford Sailing Club, 1997- present
* Straightford Men's Basketball Team, 1994-1995

A good example of a resume format that can help an applicant with little direct work experience supporting his or her candidacy. The use of a powerful quote near the top of the resume helps to compensate for a work background heavy in academic elements.

Jane Smith
123 Main St.
Mytown, State 00000
111/000-0000

"Nothing great was ever achieved without enthusiasm."
— Ralph Waldo Emerson

PROFESSIONAL PROFILE

* Skilled in financial auditing
* Performed internal audit of Computer Help Center
* Trained in statistical sampling
* Comfortable in a wide variety of operating systems
* Experienced in desktop applications
* Hands-on tax experience
* Knowledge of network accounting programs, LANs, and the Internet
* Motivated to do the job right — and with a high degree of efficiency — the first time

EDUCATION

Master's Degree, Accounting, University of WY, Casper, Wyoming; expected September, 1998
    GPA: 3.2

Bachelor's Degree in Business Administration, Marvin University, Ft. Walton Beach, FL, 1994
Honor roll; GPA 3.75

WORK EXPERIENCE

Purchasing/Receiving Clerk, Berrigan Systams, Inc., Miami, FL, June to September, 1996 (summer job)

* Planned and implemented physical inventory tracking system; dramatically increased efficiency and reduced misplaced/mismanaged stock levels.
* Placed orders for manufacturing parts with vendors; followed up on all open orders.
* Inventoried components for manufacturing and oversaw inventory security campaign, protecting stock from unauthorized access.

Computer Center Help Attendant, University of Wyoming, September 1995 to present

* Teach computer courses in spreadsheet and database software applications.
* Designed and wrote code for the Computer Center web site.
* Assist callers with questions regarding desktop applications and Internet access.

Income Tax Assistant, Volunteer Income Tax Assistance Program (Miami, FL, HealthWays Senior Center)

* Helped senior citizens complete accurate income tax forms (volunteer position).

Program Assistant, AidsWalk 1995, Miami, FL, Summer 1995

* Established payment arrangements with vendors.
* Developed outcome scenarios on Lotus 1-2-3 spreadsheet.
* Scheduled and coordinated meetings with senior event staff.

ALSO OF INTEREST

Have overseen activities involving my church's finances on a voluntary basis for the past two years, and now serve in a leadership position there.

Maintained membership records for Politics Club at Marvin University. Collected dues, assisted with bookkeeping.

Successfully trained new volunteers as part of tax preparation volunteer work.

Recipient of the Ed Berry Award for Academic Excellence, 1994.

STAFF ACCOUNTANT

Appealing to a small, entrepreneurially-oriented company? Consider this model, which features a truly powerful headline. The opening text paragraph matches the precise title of the opening in question. The resume also dispatches any possible prejudice arising from the applicant's relative youth.

Jane Smith
123 Main St.
Mytown, State 00000
111/000-0000

The RIGHT Profile

Career leading naturally to opportunity as **Staff Accountant** with **ABC Corporation**; strong work ethic, attention to detail and desire to grow with a dynamic firm. **I thrive on professional challenges.**

The RIGHT Education

Master of Accountancy, Accounting, University of Wyoming,
May 1996, GPA 3.5
B.S., Accounting, Computer Science, University of Science
and Arts of Wyoming, May 1992, GPA 3.75

The RIGHT Experience

Accountant/Assistant Office Manager
Long's Precision Machinery, Inc. Palo Alto, CA (1996-present)
Promoted to this responsible accounting position in Long's corporate facility after serving as Junior Accountant from June 1995 to June 1996. Maintain general ledgers, prepare financial reports and analysis, tax compliance, budgeting, payroll, and bank reconciliations. Perform product sales duties and provide customer support. Utilize automated accounting systems and PC in daily routine. **Cited for "accuracy and precision unparalleled in this position before your arrival" in written evaluation, 1995.**

Administrator/Bookkeeper
Sierra Foods, Richmond, CA (1994-1996)
Duties included: bookkeeping, invoice tracking, purchase orders, daily correspondence and preparation of various reports. Assisted with sales and marketing and provided customer support. **Although the youngest person on the staff, was given significant training and development duties after only six months on the job.**

Computer Programmer/Administrator (1992-1994)
University of Wyoming Business Development Program
(Contract assignment.) Programmed, debugged, and tested self-tutoring programs which were printed and assembled for disk mastering. **Personally developed procedures manual and related training materials.**

Have knowledge and experience with MS/DOS, Windows, and Macintosh
operating systems. Specific applications software includes: Lotus 1-2-3, MS Excel, MS Word, WordPerfect, Microsoft Office, Lotus Notes, and ACT! **Enjoy mastering new software tools.**

The RIGHT Outlook

"Man is born to live, and not to prepare to live." — Boris Pasternak

Here's a headline that makes it just about impossible *not* to start reading the body of the resume! The unorthodox omission of a date in the education section is justified here—the superior record of achievement more than justifies the decision to deemphasize an (un-listed) first employment experience.

Jane Smith
123 Main Street
Mytown, State 00000
111/000-0000

RESULTS
That Speak for Themselves!

Vaughn Bros. Furniture, Temple, TX 7/84-12/97
Vice President, Treasurer

Assisted the President with the development and successful execution of strategic and financial plans resulting in four consecutive record years with earnings increasing 59% on a 71% increase in sales.

* Completely restructured accounting and financial organization, eliminating redundant functions and consolidating all treasury operations, resulting in a net 10% reduction in personnel expense.

* Developed and implemented rolling sales, operations and financial forecasting systems, which made possible improvements in management information systems. Resulting benefits in on-time deliveries, reduced inventories and effective cash flow management were highlighted in company's year-end operational summary.

* Designed and implemented effective risk management/loss control policies and aggressive purchasing practices, thereby reducing worker's compensation expense 74% and saving $1.65 million over three years.

* Headed up committee that converted group health insurance to a self-insured plan for a 25% expense reduction, saving $425,000 in the first year.

Office Furniture Discounters, Inc. Somerville, MA 6/81-6/84

A manufacturer of wood and steel store fixtures with sales of $22 million, this company served major department and drug store chains from four manufacturing plants and three distribution centers.

* Converted accounting systems to new software to obtain accurate cost data and improve timeliness and reliability of financial reporting.

* Reduced average days billings outstanding in A/R from 88 days to 39 days.

* Personally restructured accounting and credit departments; revised policies and procedures for improved performance.

* Initiated a complete review of general and cost accounting systems and procedures which uncovered numerous deficiencies and inadequacies.

EDUCATION

Adams College—Quincy, MA
Bachelor of Science in Business Administration
Major: Finance; Minor: Accounting

5

Resumes That Use Unconventional Formats

How to Build a Resume That Looks Truly Distinctive

Originality does not consist in saying what no one has ever said before, but in saying exactly what you think yourself.

JAMES FITZJAMES STEPHEN

Just as there is no single correct format for a successful television or print advertisement, there is no one correct formula for a resume that makes a decision maker want to meet with you. Endorsements at the top of your document? Why not? Here are plenty of possibilities to consider.

ACCOUNTANT

Here's a resume that dramatically overcomes any potential negative reactions to an unconventional career path. The unorthodox structure and topic line selection make a knee-jerk rejection much less likely.

John Smith
123 Main St.
Mytown, State 00000
111/000-0000

AREAS OF PROFESSIONAL EXPERTISE

Auditing

Payroll

Forecasts

Budgets

Financial Statements

Financial Reporting and Management

STABILITY, EXCELLENCE, AND COMMITMENT

My **current employer is Central State University** (Portland, OR), an organization with which I have a **fifteen-year history of achievement** as both a student and employee.

I graduated from CSU with *highest honors in 1981*, attaining my B.S. in Business Administration. I was named the Steven Bell Scholar of my graduating class.

A TESTED PERFORMER

As a result of the recommendation of the head of the Department of Business Administration, I secured a temporary assignment within the office of the President of Central State University. That led to my hiring, in 1982, as a full-time Accountant within the University. **I have been named a "top performer" in my area for eleven of the last thirteen years.**

I am now eager to take what I've learned at Central State and apply it to new professional challenges.

PERFORMANCE IN RISK-INTENSIVE SETTINGS

My present duties include financial management and the reporting of state, federal and local grants, the preparation of audit work papers, and the **management of the University's $200 million investment portfolio,** a challenging and complex group of investments for which I have been granted full responsibility and praised for **"superior decision making."**

Throughout my tenure as an employee at Central State, I've focused on my commitments to **precision, accuracy, and accountability.**

The former President of Central State, Bernard Marver, described my work as **"meticulous, exacting, and consistently reliable."**

PROFICIENT IN ...

Lotus 1-2-3, Excel, Microsoft Word, Microsoft Excel, and a variety of network-related systems.

Far more important, however, is my proficiency in **delivering superior results for my employer.**

Talk about taking the direct approach! This dramatic format is calculated to make maximum impact in the shortest possible amount of time.

Jane Smith
123 Main Street
Mytown, State 00000
111/000-0000

Pressed for time?

No problem. Here's the low-down on the sharpest applicant yet for ABC's opening for an Accounting Director:

FINANCIAL PROBLEM SOLVER

ATTITUDE TOWARD NEW CHALLENGES:

I thrive on turning "high-pressure" assignments into "no-pressure" success stories.

HIGHLY SKILLED IN:

Accounts receivable, accounts payable, financial projection, financial analysis, ratios analysis

PRAISED BY:

Melvin Siegel, a former supervisor, who called my work "consistently excellent," referred to me as his "chief crisis resolver," and offered me a substantial raise not to leave the firm and start my own computer-related business.

EMPLOYMENT SUMMARY:

Web site design, various clients (2 years)

Advertising agency, director of financial operations (3 years)

Computer retailer, financial/purchasing/HR (1 year)

Educational software producer, freelance accounting system work (4 years)

Television production firm, head of accounting department (1 year)

Marketing research firm, accountant (2 years)

Extremely computer literate; fully conversant with most hardware and software

EDUCATION:

B.A. in Business Administration from West Virginia State University (1980)

Minor in Industrial Relations

A powerful resume that leads with a compelling endorsement. Word to the wise—endorsements from CEOs, presidents, and the like are not as hard to get as you might think if you build up an alliance with the person's assistant.

John Smith
123 Main Street
Mytown, State 00000
111/000-0000

"John Smith got our system up and running, and it cost less than we'd allocated. He's a results-oriented financial professional you can count on."
—Willa Rosen, CEO, American Medical Products

EXECUTIVE SUMMARY:

American Medical Products (Dover, DE)
Technology Development Consultant (8/93-11/95)

Held final responsibility for implementation of computerized accounting system at this startup operation. Came in **under budget and ahead of schedule.**

Worked with senior executives to establish **effective payment, collection, and information management procedures** for this dynamic new player in the medical products field.

Contributed **key ideas to company marketing plan.**

Attended **weekly strategy meetings** of top American Medical executives.

Called **"a major asset"** by CEO of American Medical.

Proficient in: Microsoft Office, Lotus 1-2-3, ACT!

Education:

M.B.A., Southeastern Michigan University (1993).
B.A., Business, University of Colorado (1991).

This resume effectively condenses highlights from many years of experience into a single eye-catching page. The confident, comparatively informal closing line is best reserved for prospective employers at smaller, entrepreneurial firms.

Jane Smith
123 Main Street
Mytown, State 00000
111/000-0000

Senior financial executive with a total of 21 years of experience, including 8 years with the Coverton Group and 13 years with the Freedson Motor Corporation. Pragmatic, hands-on experience within a corporate environment, with a special emphasis on project development, human resources, and maximizing efficiency within electronic data processing environments. Significant experience in cash management.

PROFESSIONAL SUMMARY

Coverton Group (New York, NY) * 1976-1984
Assistant Treasurer 1983-1984
Manager-Treasury and Taxation 1979-1983
Internal Auditor 1979-1981
General Accounting Supervisor 1976-1980

Freedson Motor Corporation (Detroit, MI) * 1984-1997
(Taiwanese manufacturing project, in cooperation with the World Bank)
Senior Director - 1990-1997
Financial & Administrative Director - 1988-1990
Assistant Financial Director - 1984-1987

Some highlights of my performance in these dynamic environments...

Coverton Group
Involved in corporate restructuring efforts; facilitated the acquisition and assimilation of Vera's Frozen Foods.

Participated in the design and implementation of a centralized cash management system operating between U.S. and Canadian divisions, minimizing conversions between currencies. This resulted in the elimination of multiple account floats, thereby reducing total debt by $468,000.

Oversaw integration of data flow from PC systems with main accounting system, thereby eliminating two levels of manual operations and improving reliability and control.

Assisted in development of income tax strategy to maximize legally permissible tax deferrals.

Freedson Motor Corporation

Identified the need for, planned and implemented an EDP information system to process stocks, sales accounting and payroll (325 employees).

Undertook research of alternative sources of spare parts and accessories to reduce dependence on one supplier and overall associated costs. This action resulted in ongoing annual savings of $216,000.

Participated actively in the review of various production and administrative cost components. Responsible for strategizing major expansion phase. The net results: a reduction of production processing and administrative costs, excluding raw material, of 31.4%.

These and other important initiatives enabled the net profit percentage ratio versus sales to improve from 8.54% (1986) to 21.22% (1991).

EDUCATION

Bachelor of Science degree, Accounting, Merseyfield College, Merseyfield, PA (1977).

To get the rest of the story—call me!

The arrow device this resume employs directly supports the dramatic headline. The resume does a superb job of reassuring the prospective employer about the applicant's ability to handle the most sensitive aspects of the position being applied for.

Jane Smith
123 Main St.
Mytown, State 00000
111/000-0000

↗ Straight to the top!

That's where this experienced, competent financial professional with experience in both nonprofit and for-profit environments has landed. I report directly to the President of the Weldon University Foundation, and meet with her three times weekly. I offer significant accounting, management, computer and communication skills — and familiarity with the job of working effectively with top executives.

WORK EXPERIENCE

Business Manager

Weldon University Foundation, Inc., West Covina, CA
Jan. 1994 - Present

↗ Report directly to President of the Foundation.

↗ Meet regularly with Board of Trustees and Board committees to develop budgets, establish sound fiscal policies, and determine best utilization of Foundation assets.

↗ Personally responsible for oversight of $19 million investment portfolio and $7 million real estate portfolio.

↗ Execute all internal and external financial reports.

↗ Supervise accounting/finance department staff (typically eight to twelve persons, not including temporary help).

Accounting Manager

Weldon University Foundation, Inc., West Covina, CA
November 1991 - January 1994

↗ Designed, produced and maintained an accounting system for affiliates of Weldon University Foundation.

↗ Developed comprehensive training module for use at both off-site affiliates and central office.

↗ Managed accounting staff of affiliates and prepared consolidating reports for Foundation.

Accounting Manager

Evergreen Savings Bank, Pismo Beach, CA
June 1990 - October 1991

↗ Managed all financial, fixed asset, and joint venture accounting activities for the savings bank and two subsidiaries.

↗ Oversaw preparation of essential internal and external reports.

↗ Tracked and evaluated bank's real estate owned (REO) properties.

Junior Accountant

Fields and Fields, Certified Public Accountants, Lompoc, CA
June 1988 - June 1990

↗ Responsible for the processing of monthly accounting data for key clients.

↗ Conducted complete analysis of all financial transactions.

↗ Oversaw quarterly payroll reports and financial statement preparation.

SOFTWARE EXPERIENCE

Spreadsheet Applications: Excel, Lotus 1-2-3, Quattro Pro

Database Applications: D-Base, Paradox, Q&A

Word Processing Applications: WordPerfect, MS Word, MultiMate

Accounting Applications: DacEasy, AccPac Plus, Quicken, M.Y.O.B., APG, Fast

Other P.C.-based applications: MS Powerpoint

EDUCATION

* University of Lompoc: M.B.A., Dec. 95
* Certified Public Accountant: May 91
* Weldon University: B.S., Accounting, Dec. 1987

CONSULTANT

Another compelling one-page summary for an applicant whose resume may serve as a business marketing tool, and whose background offers ample experience. Some experts will tell you that a multi-page resume is fine for your initial contact. My view is that your best strategy is to focus your experience onto a single page, and be prepared to provide appropriate supporting documentation and verbal summaries during your formal interview.

Jane Smith
123 Main St. / Mytown, State 00000
111/000-0000

PROFILE

Seasoned financial/accounting consultant with **deep experience in adding value to day-to-day operations and a record of success as a full-time contributor to successful businesses.**

EDUCATIONAL BACKGROUND:

B.S. in Accounting, University of Nevada, 1969
M.B.A. in Planning & Control, University of Iowa, 1971
Ph.D. in Finance & Accounting, Wyoming State University, 1974

BUSINESS EXPERIENCE:

Melvin Muller & Co. (Cincinnati, OH), Operations Research Consultant— 1969-1976
Holt Gall Flatwich (New York, NY), Consulting Division — 1976-1981
Neal Boehlert, Inc. (New York, NY), Consulting Division — 1976-1982
Independent consultant to large-scale organizations (1982 - present)

Corporate Board Positions:

Little Henry Corporation, Aurora, CO — 6 years
Belson Food Processing, Chicago, IL — 8 years
Welltech International, Austin, TX — 2 years
Albuquerque (NM) Civic Theatre —2 years
National Small Business Resource Network, New York, NY — Current

Major Consulting Engagements:

Bookwright Co.; Bird Equipment; Loss Management Corporation; RIVOLT Enterprises; The National Minority Access League; Southern States Gas & Electric; the Sacramento Trust; Mollytown Children's Clothing.

Areas of Expertise:

Budget forecasting
Credit controlling and financial controlling
Preparation and writing of major grant funding proposals and budgets
System oversight (account collections and incomplete contracts)
Selection and conversion of computerized accounting systems
Account controlling and software support
Development, preparation and analysis of accounting data
Interpretation and display of statistical information for detailed credit analyses by senior management
Litigation support-expert witness (Have provided expert evaluations in over 60 cases.)

Professional Development Programs:
Melvin Muller & Co.
    Finance for Line Managers (12 one-week seminars)
    Impact of Inflation on Decision Making (6 one-week seminars)

Holt Gall Flatwich
    Decentralized Management Planning & Control (3-day seminar)

Major Volunteer Projects Include:

In conjunction with the Minority Small Business Cooperative, General Technologies, and Wyoming State University, I oversaw the development of the Minority Entrepreneurship Program within the College of Business Administration, working closely with faculty on a volunteer basis for two years. We set up the basic curriculum, recruited minority students, developed special courses to address new needs, and offered ongoing phone and face-to-face support to those who completed the program.

Experienced with IBM Systems, Lotus 1-2-3, Macintosh Systems, Excel, MS Word, Pagemaker, Filemaker. Comfortable with web browsers, including Netscape, and HTML applications.

Email me! janesmith@brantwell.net

An intriguing, hard-to-ignore twist—putting the employment summary right up at the top, and following up with a summary of performance highlights. A superior endorsement at the bottom brings the resume to a powerful conclusion.

Jane Smith
123 Main St.
Mytown, State 00000
111/000-0000

COMPUTER EXPERTISE: Excel, Lotus, Windows 95, MS-Access, Dos, UNIX

CAREER SUMMARY:

DATE	POSITION	COMPANY
Jul 96 - present	Financial Controller	Macca Group, New Orleans, LA
Sep 95 - Jul 96	Financial Analyst	BlissOrion, New Orleans, LA
Apr 94 - Jun 95	Finance Manager	DCE DataTech, Atlanta, GA
Mar 89 - Mar 94	Financial Consultant	(Variety of U.S. clients)
Jul 87 - Feb 89	Financial Controller	Raleigh Systems, Raleigh, NC

CAREER ACHIEVEMENTS:

* Evaluated and reported project resource allocations using MS-Access.

* Responsible for financial reporting, performance summary, and internal control procedures in a variety of settings.

* Experienced in cash flow management including 3 monthly rolling forecasts, annual forecasts.

* Introduced new ledger systems resulting in significant increases in efficiency.

* Developed group cash forecasts, quarterly rolling forecasts, annual business planning.

* Have made key contributions in budgeting, compilation and consolidation of long-range planning report schedules, consolidation of monthly financial reporting package, and year-end reporting.

* Duties have included effective direct line management of finance departments.

Skilled in:

financial management
monthly reporting
statutory accounting and group reporting
cash flow management
coordination of legal matters
systems development and internal controls
liaison with external authorities such as regulatory officials and auditors

"Jane is one of the finest accounting professionals I've ever worked with."
Steve Parsons, Parsons Media Group (212/555-12

CONTROLLER

A format virtually guaranteed to stop the reader cold. It's a great way to go if you've got significant employment experience with only two employers and are looking for a way to turn that background into an asset.

Jane Smith
123 Main St.
Mytown, State 00000
111/000-0000

CPA/M.B.A. with over 10 years of experience in financial management for an information technology consulting firm, a Fortune 100 company and a public accounting firm. Past positions include:

Controller
Plant Controller
Manager of Benefits Administration
Manager of Global Reporting

Professional Summary

Resolve Corporation, 1995-1996

Controller/Business Manager - Philadelphia, PA

Resolve is the prime contractor in an information services outsourcing contract with a Fortune 500 manufacturing company. Managed organization that was responsible for accounting, human resources, purchasing, recruiting, partner relations and contracts administration of a 125-employee business unit with $18M in annual revenues.

*Essential member of startup team. Developed and implemented business infrastructure and established good business practices. **Internal audit was completed "seamlessly," according to CEO.**

*Created and implemented customized invoicing and timekeeping systems, establishing credibility with the client to allow **collection of $21M in annual revenue.**

*Improved cash management of accounts receivable to 12 days below company average, **reducing annual interest expense by $80K.**

*Analyzed operations and developed key indicators to properly manage the business. First year of operation was profitable and **exceeded forecast.**

FiberCast Company, 1980-1995

Manager, Global Reporting and Control - Danbury, CT
1992-1995

Managed technical organization that was responsible for: international accounting policy and research; analysis of international operations; analysis and reporting of foreign currency management programs; reporting of $2B in restructuring projects; and internal control training and evaluation. The organization also provided financial management for venture capital investments and supported the preparation of external reporting to shareholders.

*Created system to **analyze $120M in restructuring savings and $1.5B in restructuring reserves,** generating credibility with senior management and accountability with operating units.

*Implemented changes in the external financial reporting process, **reducing cost by $74K.**

*Selected as member of divestiture team that accomplished **sale of $900M subsidiary.**

Education

New England University - Pittsfield, MA - M.B.A. Finance, 1985.

Boston Central College - Boston, MA - B.S. Accounting and B.S. Business Administration, 1979.

"Chance favors the trained mind." — Louis Pasteur

Is there such thing as too much experience? There is if your two-page resume exhausts an already weary hiring official. Note how this resume takes a multi-page background and condenses it into a single dramatic page.

John Smith
123 Main St. / Mytown, State 00000
111/000-0000

PROFILE

* Seasoned professional with experience in all aspects of financial management.
* Experienced in accounting, business analysis, and planning in both large and medium-sized businesses.
* Superior interpersonal skills, as evidenced by consistently strong personnel reviews as a manager.
* Excellent organizational abilities.
* Capable of executing conversion from manual accounting system to computerized accounting system using varying accounting packages and computer systems.

PROFESSIONAL SKILLS

Accounting and Finance

- Budget and cash flow preparation
- Reconciliation (sub-ledgers to general ledger)
- General ledger account analyses and bank reconciliation
- Preparation and review of monthly financial statements
- Designing and implementation of integrated financial accounting system
- Completion of individual and corporate income tax returns
- Preparing year-end working papers for audited, and non-audited financial statements
- Set up new businesses with full package of financial and business information and support
- Analytical, financial and management accounting skills
- Excellent communication and group facilitation skills

Managerial Experience

- Quarterly personnel evaluations
- Coordination and supervision of employees (departmental size has ranged from 25 to 32)
- 34 of the 41 hires I recommended at Jones, Inc. were promoted within 24 months.

Computer Experience

- Skilled in upgrading computer systems to meet emerging needs.
- Intimately familiar with Lotus 1-2-3, Microsoft Office, TaxPrep, and other popular applications.

EDUCATION

Master's Degree in Business and Finance, Portland (ME) State University
Five-year program in Certified Accounting Management CMA, Sunnerston University, Winnipeg
Computer Business Application Course, Mike Smith Community College, Winnipeg

WORK EXPERIENCE

1993-Present: Controller, Jones, Inc., Chicago, IL
1991-1993: Accountant Consultant, Smithco, Chicago, IL
1990-1991: Senior Accountant, Andalou Associates, Milwaukee, WI
1984-1990: Accountant, Mel's Diners USA, Milwaukee, WI
1984: Intern, CanadaShip, Winnipeg, Manitoba, Canada

An unusual combination of employment experiences yields an unusual—
and utterly memorable—resume.

Jane Smith
123 Main St.
Mytown, State 00000
111/000-0000

I offer a unique combination of backgrounds: seven years of proven achievement with Federal Financial Corporation (New York, NY) and four years as an instructor within the Grovemont (IL) School District teaching high school juniors and seniors my "Business Basics" course. As a past supervisor once put it, **"If you can handle those kids, you can handle our clients!"**

I am proficient in Lotus 1-2-3, Excel, PowerPoint, and a wide variety of other business-related programs.

AS A FINANCIAL ADVISOR WITH FEDERAL FINANCIAL CORPORATION (1991-present), I ...

Meet with clients and develop customized presentations for them.

Develop detailed analyses of client portfolios.

Fine-tune internal presentations to be delivered to the Chief Executive Officer.

Retained 89% of current clients (ranking me among top 5% companywide).

Received "superior" rating four consecutive years.

AS A PUBLIC SCHOOL TEACHER OF THE "BUSINESS BASICS" COURSE (1988-1991), I...

Developed curriculum and selected reading materials.

Tracked daily news stories for relevant items for daily classroom discussion period.

Assembled original graphic display materials.

Was praised by parents as "innovative," "caring," and "both knowledgeable and gifted."

Was cited by superintendent of schools for "excellent interpersonal skills."

Was named "Teacher of the Year" by Grovemont School District (1990).

Let's talk soon about the best ways I can make a contribution to your organization!

An unorthodox, highly targeted resume that cannily incorporates the specifics of the open position as the applicant's "dream job."

Jane Smith
123 Main Street
Mytown, State 00000
111/000-0000

"What's your dream job?"

A challenging position as a Staff Accountant that will take advantage of my proven analytical, business, and interpersonal skills. I have developed proficiency in Lotus 1-2-3, Windows 95, World Wide Web Browsers, WordPerfect, Windows 3.1, MS Word, and MS Excel. I can speak, read, and write basic Spanish and Japanese.

"What have you done?"

DependCo
Financial and Marketing Assistant

Praised as "indispensable" upon completion of year-end review, 1996.

Responsible for planning and monitoring a wide variety of telemarketing campaigns. **Significantly increased sales effectiveness in department; net income rose by 15% in fourth quarter of 1996.**

Calculated and analyzed rates for strategic investment of company funds. **Supervisor commented that I had won "right-hand status."**

Forecasted future sales and profits of the company. Analyzed the macroenvironment for threats, opportunities, weaknesses, and strengths of the company. **Selected for personalized training program, July 1996, as preparation for strategic duties.**

Education

B.S., Finance, Portertown College, 1995

"Where do we go from here?"

Call me at the number above, or e-mail me at jane@ips.net so we can discuss the ways I can add value to your organization.

A resume unlike any other likely to cross the prospective employer's desk—yet it retains a results-oriented, professional feel throughout.

Jane Smith
123 Main Street
Mytown, State 00000
111/000-0000

IT ALL ADDS UP!

Bachelor's Degree in Mathematics (graduated 9th in my class) Dallas Technical Institute (Dallas, TX) 1989

(Plus)

Master's degree in Mathematics (graduated 3rd in my class) 1992

(Plus)

Four years of foreign markets experience as a senior executive with State Bank of Iowa, Barrister, IA, with specialty in money market dealing and foreign exchange environments (1993-1996)

(Plus)

Two years of experience as manager of a busy branch of the State Bank of Iowa (1992-1993)

(Equals)

A skilled, instinctive, informed team player with a great head for numbers and a flair for intelligent innovation. A superior financial manager ready to make instant contributions to ABC Corporation.

GENERAL LEDGER ACCOUNTANT

An excellent example of a resume that emphasizes skills to put the spotlight on potential benefits to the employer.

Jane Smith
123 Main St.
Mytown, State 00000
111/000-0000

SUMMARY: A superlative record in analysis, leadership, and communication. Strong background in finance, accounting, and financial analysis. Superior computer skills, and a long history of problem-solving success. Substantial experience in spreadsheet analysis and design. Excellent interpersonal skills.

PROFESSIONAL EXPERIENCE

ACCOUNTING

- Maintain accurate, complete general ledger; oversee related financial statement and managerial reports.
- Maintain intercompany accounts receivable between corporate office and branch office computer environments.
- Process fixed asset additions, adjustments, retirements, sales, transfers, and depreciation for financial impact.
- Prepare reports and conduct research for various departments and corporate office to ensure accurate financial information.
- Analyze and audit inventory systems.

TAXES

- Prepare monthly returns; verify for accuracy and full compliance with state and federal law.

BANK RECONCILIATION

- Responsible for analysis and reconciliation of bank accounts for local receipts, lockbox payments, and cash disbursements.
- Responsible for analysis and reconciliation of payroll disbursement ledgers and accounts.
- Verify transfers of funds.

FINANCIAL ANALYSIS

- Develop analyses of balance sheets, variance reports, and financial statements.
- Prepare financial information to demonstrate impact on budget.
- Have prepared budget and forecasts for specific accounts.
- Audit general ledger and financial statement accounts.
- Significant experience with statistical functions.

COMPUTER LITERACY

- Highly proficient in Excel, Lotus 1-2-3. Word, WordPerfect, and a host of other software applications. Well versed in Windows 95.

WORK HISTORY

Oct 1994 - Dec 1996 - SPELLRAND COMMUNICATIONS OF CENTERTOWN General Ledger
Accountant (Centertown, WA)
July 1991 - Oct 1994 - SPELLRAND COMMUNICATIONS OF SPOKANE Accountant (Spokane, WA)
June 1990 - June 1991: AMERICARD FINANCIAL SERVICES Accountant (Spokane, WA)

EDUCATION

Associate of Arts - Centertown Community College
Bachelor of Arts - Eastern Oklahoma University

Here's an example of how less really can be more! A compelling use of a concise summary of basic employment information for maximum effect. You may want to consider this approach if you're forced to submit a cold resume for an opening whose requirements are not yet well known to you.

Jane Smith
123 Main Street
Mytown, State 00000
111/000-0000

Pluses	Minuses
Significant experience in overseas offices of major U.S. corporations.	
Skilled in managing currency transactions for maximum financial benefit.	
Former employers (at least two years with each) include Magenta International, Tu-Park Corporation, the Melvin Group; in addition, worked as controller for McKay, Reed, and Misseri, a major international law firm.	
Superior written and personal references available on request; supervisor at McKay, Reed, and Misseri described me as "the Rock of Gibraltar" and "a company superstar."	
B.A., International Business Management - Grace State University	
Fluent in German, Spanish, and French; conversant in Japanese.	
Proficient in all major computer applications.	
Ready, eager and willing to improve ABC Company's bottom line.	

Here, the resume highlights are emphasized in callout boxes that are
virtually impossible to overlook.

Jane Smith
123 Main St.
Mytown, State 00000
111/000-0000
email: janesmith@mynet.com

I am an experienced portfolio manager with a strong background in derivatives, risk management, mortgage backed securities and CMOs.

EXPERIENCE

USABANK, New York, NY
1996-present
Manage $3.5 billion portfolio including CMOs, MBS Pass-throughs, and Corporate Bonds in a highly analytical A/L management environment.

Evaluate alternatives to hedge mortgage servicing portfolio, including tax, accounting, transfer pricing and regulatory issues. Created prepayment swap contract which facilitated risk transfer from mortgage lending division to Corporate Treasury; executed $15 billion in national. Using Value At Risk (VAR) executed Super PO transactions to hedge mortgage servicing. Recommended interim hedge solution using exchange traded futures and options which allowed bank to bid on large servicing portfolio while minimizing risk until permanent hedge was executed.

> **Assisted in transaction that achieved substantial tax savings; presented to and won approval from senior management committee.**

Identified and executed opportunity to efficiently hedge the Bank's short option position by buying mispriced options in the form of putable corporate bonds.

> **Estimated savings: $1.7 million.**

> **Created intranet Web page for company work group.**

ILLINOIS SAVINGS, Chicago, IL
1993-1994
Chief Investment Officer

Responsible for risk management using $600 million portfolio of derivatives including swaps, caps, floors, CMO swaps and swaptions.

> **Implemented new software to enhance analytical capabilities and allow for seamless integration of database and analytics.**

Recommended low-cap ARM loan program which increased production 425% while providing market level returns after hedge costs (interest rate corridors) as well as profitable sale execution. Pricing was followed by many competitors.

> **Praised for "significant improvements in department efficiency" by senior executive within the firm.**

STATE OF ILLINOIS BANK OVERSIGHT BOARD, Chicago, IL
1992-1993
Capital Markets Analyst

Analyzed capital markets issues including interest rate risk, divestitures and other restructurings.

Duties included: evaluating hedge programs; analyzing financial instruments on legal, structural, and tax issues.

> **Presented findings to senior management and board; praised for "keenly observed, accurate,**

I hold an M.B.A. degree from Brentwell University (1992) and a bachelor's degree in Accounting from Masterson College (1990).

A savvy, nothing-but-business Assumption section gets this resume started with a bang! Applicants targeting resumes toward entry-level openings must, as a general rule, be ready to take bold steps along these lines.

Entry-Level Finance Position

John Smith
123 Main Street
Mytown, State 00000
111/000-0000

ASSUMPTION:

I believe I can help your company achieve its goals by making contributions in an entry-level position within your financial department that requires persistence, deadline orientation, strong number sense, and a high level of accuracy.

TOOLS:

I hold a Business Administration degree with an emphasis in international business from Central Pomona University **(3.5/4.0 grade point average).**

I have extensive experience with Excel, Lotus 1-2-3, Access, Powerpoint, and WordPerfect. I am comfortable working within a 10-key environment and type 50+ words per minute.

BACKGROUND:

AmeriStay Hotels (national chain) January 1997-present

I currently work as an Auditor for the Anytown branch of this $55 million national hotel chain. I'm responsible for maintaining accurate totals of each evening's business and submitting double-checked reports to my supervisors. My duties also include front desk responsibilities, which demand patience, flexibility, and the ability to interact pleasantly and promptly with customers.

I've received positive personnel evaluations during each of my two salary reviews at AmeriStay; the last evaluation described me as **"a real asset to the hotel, the kind of person who adds a lot to the organization."**

Leading the resume with an "I" statement isn't, perhaps, the most orthodox way to get the job done. Neither, for that matter, is incorporating, on the back of the resume, three or four concise excerpts from your most enthusiastic written references. But when you know the competition is tough, you may need to take dramatic steps like these.

John Smith
123 Main St.
Mytown, State 00000
111/000-0000

I have assembled extensive (and enthusiastic!) written references;
see excerpts on the reverse side of this resume,
or call me at the number above for the complete text.

Professional Profile

A committed financial professional who combines analytical/quantitative skills, strong leadership abilities, superior written communication and public speaking skills, and deep levels of computer software mastery. (Proficient in: Microsoft Office [including Excel]; Lotus 1-2-3; ACT; and many other programs.)

Professional Experience

AMALAGAMATED FINANCIAL CORPORATION
Chicago, IL
Senior Auditor (6/95 - present)

* Executed financial audits with heavy emphasis on evaluation of procedures and controls.
* Prepared financial statements. Analyzed financial reports and budget.
* Isolated instances of waste, fraud, and abuse totaling **$650,000,** and made appropriate recommendations that prevented future overexpenditures in relevant areas.

SUPERIOR PRODUCTS INC.
Albuquerque, NM
Special Assistant to the Vice President of Finance (1/94 - 6/95)

* Was responsible for all financial functions within the corporation: banking, accounts receivable and payable, and taxes.
* Kept detailed records of sales and balanced all books monthly.
* Installed and managed accounting department's new computer system.

ADVANCED TECHNOLOGY CORPORATION
San Juan, PR
Senior Accounting Consultant (6/94 - 12/93; contract assignment)

* Oversaw all cost accounting, tax accounting and data processing functions for this startup firm.
* Selected all hardware, software, and training tools.
* Gave final approval to in-house technical manuals.
* Sat in on weekly Executive Committee meetings.
* Offered advice on all aspects of the business during critical seven-month launch period; company is now a viable operation that has closed in the black three of the past four years.

BRENTCAL CORPORATION
Mill Valley, CA
Regional Manager (9/92 - 3/94)

* Oversaw all marketing and customer service activities; led region to **15% increase in profitability over previous year.**
* Recruited and trained sales representatives.
* Developed all sales forecasts and preliminary budgets.

Education

University of New Mexico at Albuquerque, Albuquerque, NM
B.S. December 1992, Accounting, Major GPA: 3.7 (Overall GPA: 3.6.)

Personal

Quick study; cooperative; team player.

STAFF ACCOUNTANT

The problem: You have to demonstrate financial management skills you have yet to use on the job. The solution: Highlight college coursework that directly relates to the job you're after, and bolster your cause with dramatic endorsements.

John Smith
123 Main Street
Mytown, State 00000
111/000-0000

Master of Business Administration (December 1996) Carwell College, Hackensack, NJ. Concentration: Finance and Management

Relevant Coursework:

Financial Management * International Management Practice * Security Analysis * Taxes as Basis for Managerial Decision * International Corporate Finance * Total Quality Management *

Praised as "a born financial problem solver." (Professor Norm Wellstone)

Bachelor of Business Administration (March 1996) University of Greenville, Greenville, NC. Major: Accounting

Relevant Coursework:

Advanced Accounting * International Business * Internal Auditing and Control * Risk Management and Insurance * Seminar in Managerial Accounting * Seminar in Tax Problems *

Made Dean's List four times.

Experience:

WaiJo Monetary, Ltd. Tokyo, Japan
March 1993 - February 1994

Staff Accountant

Performed accounting functions: journal entries, bank reconciliation, and trial balance. * Prepared monthly financial reports submitted to the Bank of Tokyo. * Calculated tax payable and prepared tax documents for company's portfolio. * Helped to prepare financial statements.

Computer Skills:

WordPerfect, Word, Excel, Powerpoint, Access, Lotus 1-2-3. Well versed in Internet applications.

Also of Interest:

45 hours in Interpersonal Communications Training
Elected Treasurer, University of Greenville Accounting Society

An already compelling resume is made even more impressive by the inclusion of a unique feature: references on the *rear* of the document! These should take the form of three to four concise verbatim paragraphs that sing your praises, and include appropriate contact information from the people you've quoted.

Jane Smith
123 Main St
Mytown, State 00000
111/000-0000

I am committed to the goal of obtaining full-time employment as an analyst or trader with ABC Corporation.

EDUCATION

University of Nevada - Reno
Master of Science in Business, May 1996, Finance; Quantitative
Math Finance Track, GPA Major 3.9/4.0 Overall 3.5/4.0
Independent study project after graduation: ABC Corporation's Trading Operations, 1990-1995

College of the West, Denver, CO
Bachelor of Science, June 1994, Mathematics and Finance, GPA 3.8/4.0

EXPERIENCE

Risk Management Consultant
Portland Energy Associates - Portland, OR
July 1995 - June 1996

Assisted in managing the risk of Portland's open and hedged *Petroleum Development* and *Clean Coal* positions.
Currently finalizing a daily financial position and reporting system.
Involved in the valuation of derivative products in various energy markets.

Assistant Pricing Analyst
Fidelity Twin Insurance - Appleton, WI (Semester breaks, 1992-1994)

Provided forecasts, projections, analysis and support to management on pressing financial issues. **This work subsidized part of my college tuition expenses.**
Created an array of innovative financial report formats for senior management personnel.
Combed company and industrywide data to develop an analysis and determine the effects of insurance regulatory actions.
Developed extensive experience in pricing, policy language analysis and regulatory compliance.
My college studies featured extensive work in derivatives and related fields. (See reverse side of this resume for a full class listing.)

SKILLS

Computer Languages - C, C++, Fortran, Pascal, Visual Basic, Basic, Java, HTML
Computer Applications - Microsoft Office 95, Lotus 1-2-3, Quattro Pro, many others

Here's a great way to separate yourself from the crowd—lead with your aptitudes, rather than an employment objective or lengthy professional summary. If the rest of your resume supports this summary, this format can be quite effective.

John Smith
123 Main Street
Mytown, State 00000
111/000-0000

Aptitudes:

Goal oriented
Hardworking
Self-starting
Conscientious team player

Education:

1993-Present-Delta University School of Management
B.B.A. degree in Business Finance expected May, 1997.

Selected as one of thirty students to travel to Philippines and help rebuild poverty-stricken communities following typhoon. Duties included bookkeeping and fundraising for sponsoring organization; personally responsible for the management of over twenty thousand dollars in donations.

Experience:

Richter, Forest, and Green (San Francisco, CA)
1996-present

Aid analysts in determining ratings on stocks watched by investment executives. Develop reports on performance of companies in the technology sector; identify key trends and highlight areas of poor or superior performance. Assist traders in creating a market for particular stocks.

Cutlow and Price, Inc. (Oakland, CA)
Summer 1996

Composed trade reports detailing the buyer, price, and amount of stock traded. Also wrote up commission reports summarizing various firms' monthly stock transactions. Other duties included serving as a floor runner on floor of Pacific Trading Exchange.

TriState Information Center (San Francisco, CA)
Summer 1995

Selected as intern for the Senior Vice President of the Sales and Marketing Department. Responsible for organizing networking events that attracted three to five hundred tristate area business owners. Prepared reports concerning nonrenewal trends in Association membership.

Skills:

Proficient in Word, WordPerfect 6.0, Lotus 1-2-3, Quattro Pro, Excel, ACT!, Paradox

6

Resumes That Take a Bold Graphic Approach
Jazz Things Up Visually

Audacity, more audacity, and always audacity!
GEORGES JACQUES DANTON

Anyone who tells you that presentation doesn't influence the way employers evaluate resume content is living in a bygone employment era. Here's a rundown on the best ways to give your resume a graphic makeover.

The talking points in this resume receive special emphasis. Note, too, the personalized appeal that incorporates the author's e-mail address. Don't use this approach unless you check your e-mail regularly!

Jane Smith
123 Main St.
Mytown, State 00000
111/000-0000

A CPA with superior software skills in: Lotus 1-2-3, Microsoft Office, ACT!, and many other programs in both Windows and Macintosh environments. Excellent interpersonal abilities and office management experience.

Professional Experience

9/94-5/96
Accountant: Spellman Associates, Cleveland, OH

* Output accurate general, payroll, accounts receivable/payable ledgers; developed financial statements, year-end closings and bonuses.

* Prepared corporate/individual income tax returns.

* Provided complete bookkeeping service on a monthly basis for over two dozen commercial clients.

> **I received "above average" or "excellent" ratings in three consecutive salary review periods at Spellman.**

4/92-7/94
Accounting Manager: Mehitabel Perspectives, San Mateo, CA

* Increased output despite reduced staff.

* Designed and implemented transition from paper to a fully integrated computer accounting system.

* Responsible for accounts payable/receivable, billing/invoicing, collections, payroll, financial statements, petty cash, sales tax and payroll tax returns.

* Produced several monthly budgeting and analytical reports.

> **My supervisor at Mehitabel wrote that I was responsible for "significant increases in accuracy, efficiency, and productivity" within the company.**

5/90-3/92
Staff Accountant: Melville & Company, Santa Cruz, CA

* Provided bank reconciliation and bookkeeping services including basic general ledger, payroll, accounts receivable/payable, financial statement preparation.
* Prepared corporate income, payroll, and property tax returns.

> **This was a part-time position I held while working toward my degree at UCSC; I was offered a full-time position at Melville in March 1992, but elect, to accept an offer from Mehitabel (above).**

Education:

University of California at Santa Cruz
B.S. in Business Administration - Accounting, 1992

> **My research indicates I can deliver quantifiable positive results for your organization. E-mail me for more information! My address: janesmith@hypernet.com**

ACCOUNTING SUPERVISOR

A creative, appropriate way to add visual appeal to your candidacy. The objective, of course, is to draw attention to material of greatest interest to the prospective employer.

Jane Smith
123 Main St.
Mytown, State 00000
111/000-0000

Professional Highlights

WorldTel Group
(Milton, Massachusetts)
Accounting Supervisor
March 1996 - Present

As one of six regional accounting supervisors at this dynamic new telecommunications firm, I know what it takes to get good results from a team, and am skilled in training and oversight of all aspects of financial reporting, filing, and review, including:

*Payroll
*Budgets
*Forecasts
*Accounts payable
*Accounts receivable
*Monthly reports
and reconciliations

KD Personnel Agency, Inc.
(Worcester, MA)
Accounting Manager
May 1995 - March 1996

Personally responsible for the execution of all accounting and finance functions at this fast-paced, high-growth agency specializing in the temporary placement of experienced data entry professionals. Prepared budgets and forecasts with the president of the company and oversaw payroll, accounts payable, accounts receivable, budgets, and a variety of reports summarizing key financial data.

* Met twice weekly with head of the firm.
* Prepared financial information essential for bank loan that made company expansion possible.
* Overhauled collection procedures; reduced bad debt by 17% in a single year.

Coble County Care Associates
(Vera Tedea, FL)
Accounting Technician
June 1989 - May 1995

Responsible for all tasks relating to accounting and financial reporting for this mid-sized nursing home. Generated state and federal quarterly tax reports, state sales tax reports, and other essential data summaries.

* Cited for "exemplary" performance in 1994 performance review.
* Certified in State of Florida Health Care Facility Accounting Procedures (January 1990).

Education

Vera Tedea Technical Institute
Graduate, 1989
Diplomas in Accounting/Data Processing; graduated with highest honors.

Skills

Proficient in Lotus 1-2-3, WordPerfect, Windows, Windows 95, Computerized Accounting, QuickBooks Pro, Microsoft Office. Experienced in mainframe and network environments. Familiar with installing and uninstalling software packages.

I respond quickly to all e-mail queries. Contact me at ...
janesmith@rightconnect.com

A fairly straightforward approach as far as content is concerned—but note the powerful formatting of the contact information!

111/000-0000 **Mytown, State 00000** **123 Main St.** **Jane Smith**

PROFESSIONAL PROFILE

I have a demonstrated record of success within fast-paced accounting environments. For the last six years, I have served as an effective, innovative accounting manager at the regional offices of one of the nation's top restaurant chains, Master Burger International.

EMPLOYMENT HISTORY

Master Burger International (Northeastern Regional Headquarters), Boston, MA
December 1994 - Present
Supervisor-Accounting

Accounting Responsibilities: Location Controller. Maintain general ledger and fixed asset activity, supervise accounts payable, accounts receivable and inventory control, maintain manufacturing costs data, and prepare financial reports for transmission to Master Burger International.

MIS Responsibilities: Administrator for plant LAN. Location MIS contact for remote connections to Master Burger locations. Responsible for computer hardware troubleshooting and maintenance.

Purchasing Responsibilities: Location Sr. Buyer. Responsible for purchasing all materials needed for administration, maintenance and production at Boston facility. Responsible for maintaining proper vendor controls as outlined by Master Burger policies.

TaxCo
Cambridge, MA
October 1992 - December 1994.
Staff Accountant

Responsible for initial setup and maintenance of company books for various clients, including general ledger, accounts payable, accounts receivable, fixed assets and payroll. Also responsible for bank account reconciliation, financial statements, payroll returns (quarterly & annual), and state and federal tax returns (individual and business).

Chamber Health Insurance Plans
November 1990 - June 1992
Plan Administrator

Responsible for administration of small business insurance plan consisting of 300+ employer groups. Successfully carried out detail-sensitive assignments, including: accounts receivable, accounts payable, invoicing, bank reconciliation, commission calculation and processing.

Health Insurance Services
October 1987 - October 1990
Staff Accountant

Responsible for initial setup and maintenance of company books. Successfully carried out detail-sensitive assignments, including: accounts receivable, accounts payable, payroll, financial statements and payroll tax returns. Designed various spreadsheet programs to improve invoicing procedure.

EDUCATION

Walnut Grove University, Walnut Grove, MA.

Currently pursuing a **Masters in Business Administration**. Concentrations in Finance and International Business.

Central Boston College, Boston, MA

Bachelor of Science in Business Administration **(Honors)**

Brookline Technical Institute, Brookline, MA

Associate Degree in Applied Science of Accounting **(Honors)**

AND THERE'S MORE!

Fluent in German and Spanish and, for that matter, in Lotus 1-2-3 and all Microsoft Office programs.

Another simple but memorable graphic device. Most up-to-date word processors allow
you to import special symbols like the one employed in this resume.

John Smith
123 Main St.
Mytown, State 00000
111/000-0000

"THE OF THE DEPARTMENT!" — (Supervisor, July 1997)

Professional Experience:

Bookkeeper, Stanway, Inc. Atlanta, GA 1992-present

Total daily sales sheets, cost out invoices, evaluate totals and operating practices by using Lotus
1-2-3 and Microsoft Office. Selected as departmental "Employee of the Month" three times within
fourteen-month period.

Bookkeeper, Overlook Associates, Decatur, GA 1991-1992

Handled bank reconciliations and sales tax adjustments; coded and input checks; maintained
journal entries. Processed tax returns. Provided support for major reorganization of accounting
system. Learned new systems and procedures quickly and completely during transfer period.

Bookkeeper, MallWorks Inc., Omaha, NE 1990-1991

Handled general ledger and accounts receivable for over 300 accounts; processed bank reconciliations for three accounts, oversaw weekly payroll. Handled debits and credits for both receivables and payables. Shifted easily between formal job duties and unforeseen assignments at this
six-person startup.

OTHER ACTIVITIES:

Treasurer for the Central Atlanta chapter of Samariteens. I combine my volunteer accounting
work with this organization with once-a-week stints assisting with mailings and phone work.

Education: Red Hill University, Baton Rouge, LA
Bachelor of Science in Consumer and Family Economics, June 1990

Check out the innovative use of the display face in this resume—and the summary of
Traits for Success at the bottom.

John Smith
123 Main Street
Mytown, State 00000
111/000-0000

bookkeeper/accountant

experience

Cyclone Co., Ottawa
June 1996 - present

My responsibilities include:
Establishing and managing the accounts of a number of affiliated companies.
Expertly processing accounts payable, accounts receivable, general ledger, deposits, and monthly
bank reconciliations.
Preparing statement of cash flows and other vital reports for senior management.
Assembling all required documentation and correspondence.

Interior Finance Ministry, Nairobi, Kenya
May 1994 - May 1996

I was in charge of US$160 million annual funds. Duties included:
Capital project coordination and management
Financial analysis
Financial forecasting and planning
Preparation of annual operating and capital budgets
Project accounting and preparation of financial statements and other management reports

In addition, I also supervised four accounting clerks and two administrative assistants. I was honored with Public Service Awards of Excellence three times during my two years in Kenya.

The Inside - An Electronic Health Care Magazine
April 1993 - May 1994

Was fully responsible for all financial functions of this nonprofit organization, with duties encompassing:

Accounts receivable	Accounts payable
General ledger	Payroll
Preparation of budgets and year-end financial statements	

skills

A/R, A/P, G/L, and Payroll	Accounting: AccPac and QuickBooks
Spreadsheets: Lotus 1-2-3 and Excel	Word Processing: WordPerfect and Word

traits for success

self-starting	accountable
results-oriented	diligent

BUSINESS MANAGER, NONPROFIT ENVIRONMENT

The headings and text in this resume emphasize a real-world look and feel that can't help putting your accomplishments in a positive light. The effect is relatively easy to execute if you have access to a good collection of fonts for use with your computer.

Jane Smith
123 Main St.
Mytown, State 00000
111/000-0000

AREAS OF EXPERTISE INCLUDE:

BUDGETING
SERVICE CONTRACTING
PROCUREMENT
COST ALLOCATION
RESPONSIBILITY ACCOUNTING
HIGH-EFFICIENCY OPERATION WITHIN NONPROFIT FINANCIAL ENVIRONMENTS
FACILITIES MANAGEMENT INFORMATION SYSTEMS

PROFESSIONAL EXPERIENCE

DIRECTOR, BUSINESS OPERATIONS
Centralside Hospital Facilities Management Department (Toledo, OH)
March 1993 - present

* Develop, manage and review budget for department.
* Personally responsible for establishment and review of internal controls.
* Implement responsibility accounting system.
* Manage cost accounting, materials, M.I.S. and finance and budget staff in all business areas.
* Responsible for control and processing of financial transactions ($74 million).
* Responsible for overseeing all accounting and financial procedures in department.
* Oversee and coordinate implementation of facilities management system (FMS).
* Establish and implement departmental productivity guidelines and principles.
* Train staff of four in budget and accounting procedures.

MANAGER, ACCOUNTING AND FINANCE
Bellworth Hospital Business Office (Cincinnati, OH)
July 1990 - March 1993

* Manage accounting and finance staff in all financial functions.
* Responsible for the control and processing of all financial transactions ($30 million).
* Produce financial statement, P&L, balance sheet for Director.
* Coordinate the annual budget preparation and submission.
* Perform internal audits.
* Act as financial advisor to managers.
* Teach Bellworth accounting and budget procedures course to staff members.

BUSINESS MANAGER/AUDITOR/ACCOUNTANT
Masonic Service Association of Ohio and Indiana (Dayton, OH)
April 1988 - July 1990

* Performed regular audits in regional elder care facilities.
* Managed staff of sixteen bookkeepers.
* Prepared consolidated financial statements for chain of nursing homes and social service groups ($8 million) for director.
* Served as liaison with federal and state government authorities; developed and filed accurate, timely financial reports.
* Revamped bookkeeping procedures, resulting in "significant increases in efficiency and cost savings" (according to executive director).

AUDITOR/ACCOUNTANT
Harrison and Cantwell, Certified Public Accountants (Cincinnati, OH)
June 1985 - April 1988

* Initially, worked part-time auditing manufacturers.
* Recruited for full-time position, June 1985.
* Analyzed financial data and assisted in preparation of financial statements for various businesses.

KLEBERG UNIVERSITY (Dayton, OH)
Bachelor of Science, Business Administration
Made Honors list four times.

BUYER

Considering powerful supporting graphics or illustrations? Don't overdo it! Note how a single tasteful graphic draws the whole resume together.

Jane Smith
123 Main Street
Mytown, State 00000
111/000-0000

Overview

A dedicated, team-oriented financial professional with significant depth of experience and a wide variety of computer skills, including all popular spreadsheets and word processors.

Possess Exceptional Skills in . . .

Inventory Control

Team Building

Merchandising

Buying

Network Systems Management

Computer Systems

Experience

Hobomok Department Stores
9/87 to present

Buyer/Merchandiser/Manager

Headed up the sales and merchandising activities of a three-million-dollar apparel and home furnishings department. Purchased over 40 separate subdivisions, maintaining 93% in-stock levels and staying within 6% of inventory allowance. Thirteen sales and sales support associates reported to me. Cited at annual regional conference as the "most gifted inventory management specialist in the Northeast."

* Consistently identified and highlighted merchandise that produced above-average sales volume.
* Assumed leadership role in two store openings that were 100% complete within deadline, above standard and within budget.
* Installed and provided technical training on buyer workstations.
* Spearheaded advertising campaign that produced largest single sales day record in our district.
* Used analytical, organizational and team-building skills to bring sales and profits to the top 15% out of 26 stores in our district.

Carl's Club, U.S.A.
12/83 to 9/87

Buyer/Merchandiser/Manager

As a manager for this national members-only retailer, I made a habit of exceeding sales and profit goals.

*   Set record unit sales by planning assortments and purchasing merchandise.

*   Launched customer credit program that generated 100%+ increases over previous efforts.

*   Developed highly accurate forecasts for sales and inventory levels.

*   Established and executed marketing and promotional plans that generated double-digit gains.

Education

PCH University, Portland, OR

Bachelor of Science, 1982

Major in Social Science

An unforgettable marriage of a catchy headline and a vivid image—both of which tie into the applicant's experience. This resume holds back information for maximum effect and sparks the "tell me more" instinct that leads to interviews.

Jane Smith
123 Main St.
Mytown, State 00000
111/000-0000

I CAN HELP TAKE YOUR DEPARTMENT TO THE HEIGHTS!

* My **twenty-three years of accounting and data management achievement** includes stints with ...

U. S. Navy (Various airborne units) 1975 - 1979
Smith, Benson, and Union (Chicago) 1982 - 1984
Melton, Creamer, and Weiss (Chicago) 1984 - 1987
Vanson & Associates (New York) 1987 - present

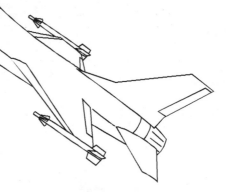

* Professional Memberships and Activities

Certified Public Accountant - New York
American Institute of CPAs
New York Society of CPAs
Institute of Management Accountants

* I have a **record of quantifiable success** in the following areas:

Auditing and accounting   Small business consulting
Cost accounting   Corporate taxation

Among the 357 clients for whom I have worked over the course of my career are those in the following industries:

Construction contractors
Manufacturing
Nonprofit organizations
Trucking and transportation

Clients have praised my work as "unimpeachable," "relentlessly accurate," "thorough," "reliable," and "consistently associated with streamlining maneuvers that have resulted in lower operating costs."

I'd like to learn more about how my skills and past achievements might match with your organization. Please contact me at the number above, or e-mail me at
janesmith@connectnet.com

The check mark has all kinds of positive connotations in a business setting.
It's put to excellent use here!

John Smith
123 Main St.
Mytown, State 00000
111/000-0000

FINANCIAL DATA MANAGEMENT PROFESSIONAL

I have worked for the past nine years in the finance/accounting area; my responsibilities now include managing a Novell network with over 270 users. I have extensive spreadsheet and analytical experience. I have led a variety of projects from accounting software implementations to network installations. I have significant experience in process analysis and planning, and offer superior network and PC software experience:

✓Novell	✓DOS
✓Excel	✓Microsoft Word
✓Lotus 1-2-3	✓WordPerfect
✓Microsoft Access	✓Lotus Freelance
✓Windows 95	✓Lotus Notes

Professional Highlights:

Morton County Community College District (Smithtown, RI)

Business Operations / Data Processing Manager (1992-present)

My current responsibilities include management of accounting and information technology systems and, since 1996, a staff of four. **The accounting office is responsible for the maintenance of all college financial records.** This includes purchasing, accounts receivable, accounts payable, cashiering functions, and accounting for grant disbursements. The staff I supervise maintains an extensive computer network, and provides support, installation, maintenance, and evaluation of all hardware and software systems.

The unit I oversee also provides support to the office of the Vice President of Central Services for budget analysis, development and management. We also support all college auxiliary and contracted services.

My unit received primarily "exceptional" ratings from surveyed users.

Budget Analysis/Financial Reporting Specialist (1989-1992)

My duties included development, analysis, oversight and reporting of all operational budgets for the District. I developed a high degree of competency within mainframe and microcomputer environments, and served as the risk manager for the District, with full responsibility for oversight of the property/casualty insurance portfolio.

I was categorized as "above average" or "superior" in each of my performance evaluations during this period.

I hold an MBA degree from Central Arkansas State University (1988) and a Bachelor of Science degree in Accounting from Foundation University (1986).

Can you really put your name at the *bottom* of the resume? You can if you provide a suitably powerful, targeted opening, as this one does. By following this approach, you subtly pose the question: "Who is this superstar?"

Objective

To use my education and experience to enhance organizational effectiveness and client relations at ABC Health Corporation as financial administrator. I offer:

* Broad-based knowledge of the inner workings/management of health administration arenas.

* Extensive knowledge of the financial management tools that allow facilities to operate smoothly.

* Experience in working with team members on a variety of levels, in a timely manner, regardless of obstacles encountered in busy operations.

Experience

South Bay Community Center
8/96 -12/96 - Administrator in Training Internship

Responsibilities included management, finance, marketing and all aspects of quality resident care (home health, assisted living and skilled nursing). Assisted the Certified Nursing Home Administrator with accounting procedures, budget and market analysis, cash flow preparation, HMO's / third party payments, and employee wages and benefits packages, and gained a thorough knowledge of Medicare guidelines.

Therapeutic Solutions
12/95 - Present

Process Medicare/Medicaid billing statements for approval by the administrator. Utilize ICD diagnostic codes on a daily basis. Cited for "operational excellence" (June 1996).

Skills

Superior interpersonal skills. Competent in Excel, Lotus 1-2-3, and other popular financial management programs. Adapt quickly and easily to customized computer software programs.

Education

Currently pursuing a Master's Degree in Health Administration from the University of the Everglades. B.S. Degree in Health Science from the University of the Everglades (1995); Dean's List.

Jane Smith * 123 Main Street * Mytown, State 00000 * 111/000-0000

Going up! The witty use of the "rising line" logo supports a powerful personal summary
and a series of compelling benefit bullets.

Jane Smith
123 Main Street
Mytown, State 00000
111/000-0000

 An experienced, versatile general manager with a documented track record of substantial success in financial and general management, P&L management, sales, marketing, analysis and strategic and operational planning.

KEY ACCOMPLISHMENTS

190% increase in production output in 4 years.
65% revenue and 43% market share increase in 4 years.
40% manufacturing staff reduction in 4 years.

 "Creative, field-tested" strategist with seven years of experience at MaxCo (Oakland, CA) as Senior Financial Manager; specialize in maximizing profitability by making the very most of new market opportunities.

* Launched new division with first-year profits of $615,000.
* Achieved $16 million revenue increase in 4 years by increasing distribution channels and product line extensions.
* Generated 7% annual revenue increase by developing and expanding international business.
* Created new profit center that generated $610,000 in annual processing fees.

 Proven ability to deliver significant cost savings.

* Saved $2.6 million annually through purchase price negotiations.
* Achieved $300,000 annual freight savings through detailed freight study and contract negotiations.
* Saved $1.4 million annually by improving staff productivity and implementing new technologies.

 A superior performer who can dramatically increase ABC Corporation's efficiency and profitability in the following areas:

Benefits administration
Promotion and advertising
Brand launch
Personnel

EDUCATION

MBA, Marketing (1982); BS, Finance, Magna Cum Laude (1979)
Ventara State University, Atlanta, GA

FINANCIAL MANAGER—TAXATION FOCUS

An intriguing example of a resume that wins visual interest through the formatting of headlines.

Jane Smith
123 Main St.
Mytown, State 00000
111/000-0000

Profile

Seasoned financial professional eager to make a contribution to a dynamic, results-oriented organization from a senior level financial management position in taxation.

Experience

WEST VIRGINIA UNIVERSITY, Charleston, WV
Assistant Professor of Accounting
September 1987 - Present

Regularly accorded ratings in the top 15% through anonymous student evaluations. Teach principles of accounting, cost accounting, intermediate accounting, advanced accounting, corporate and partnership taxation, and managerial tax planning. Elected as Faculty Senate representative.

CERTIFIED PUBLIC ACCOUNTANT, Charleston, WV
Consulting services
September 1986 - Present

Provide financial solutions for dozens of businesses ranging in size from $250,000 to $75M in annual gross income. Perform accounting, bankruptcy, and tax advisory services for several large and small businesses. Client issues have included fixed asset and lease accounting, corporate reorganizations and liquidations, consolidated tax returns, inventory management, interperiod tax provisions, accounting systems and microcomputer applications.

REVEILLE COMPANY, Falls Church, VA
Corporate Tax Director and Assistant Treasurer
March 1985 - August 1986

Brought on board to provide leadership and insight during most challenging period in this company's history. Established new tax department with complete responsibility for all tax matters. Coordinated relocation of other accounting functions. Administered Corporate Payroll Department. Took part in developing 10-year business plan submitted to lenders during restructuring negotiations. Negotiated with prospective purchasers of discontinued business segments.

LANGSTON MANUFACTURING COMPANY, Richmond, VA
Corporate Tax Manager
April 1982 - March 1985

Acted as liaison with all tax authorities. Personally responsible for all elements of corporate tax compliance, planning and research functions. Determined income tax provision. Forecasted and scheduled tax payments. Controlled federal, state and foreign tax audits. Developed extensive data processing applications. Analyzed potential mergers and acquisitions, calculating tax consequences of each.

CORELCO CORPORATION, Atlanta, GA
Tax Accountant
May 1979 - March 1982

Prepared federal, state and foreign income tax returns. Assisted in settlement of income tax audits. Supervised junior tax accountants.

Education

B.S. 1978 VIRGINIA STATE UNIVERSITY
Major: Accounting

M.S. 1990 WEST VIRGINIA STATE UNIVERSITY
Major: Taxation

Memberships and Community Service:

Certified Public Accountant since 1983.
American Institute of Certified Public Accountants
United Way of Southern West Virginia, Finance Committee

Superior references available on request.

When the layout in a resume like this is targeted to match the product of the prospective employer in question, the effect can be quite powerful. Note the "product guarantee" at the top.

Your New
Head of Financial Operations

John Smith
Accountant
123 Main St. Mytown, State 00000 * 111/000-0000

YOUR SATISFACTION WITH THIS PRODUCT IS GUARANTEED!

(Simply notify me of your decision within 30 days after any company-mandated probationary period has passed, and I will cheerfully submit my resignation.)

PROFESSIONAL EXPERTISE

★ Proven experience in both for-profit and non-profit environments; comfortable working with team members to develop radical improvements in computer, accounting and management systems.

★ Extensive background in computers and in-depth understanding of a wide variety of businesses.

★ Maximize and expand areas of profitability.

★ Implementation and conversion of over 120 different accounting systems; maximized efficiency of end-users with hands-on training.

I am experienced in a wide variety of financial and database software environments. Here are just a few:

★ Lotus 1-2-3
★ Excel
★ QuickBooks
★ Access
★ PowerCount
★ Your Money
★ Quicken

... and a great many more in both mainframe and PC environments.

EMPLOYMENT HISTORY

1995-present
United Plan Care and Outreach Services, Elmwood, WA
Head of Financial Operations

Supervised a staff of 16 in the accounting and computer departments of a non-profit organization with a budget of $6.5 million. Turned around an accounting department that had no regular monthly financial reporting, an audit that was over nine months behind schedule, and low morale due to frequent department head changes. Was assigned personal responsibility for the computer department, which used an undocumented and malfunctioning system. Solved the situation with a cost-saving transition to better equipment and software. Consolidated a good team by training and promoting staff from within the departments.

1993-1995
Glenwood, Mars and Doar Data and Accounting Services, Seattle, WA
Senior Administrative Specialist

Managed staff of seven; oversaw all administrative functions of a four-partner CPA office. Developed client relationships and marketed company services. Established policies and systems, offered input on important management decisions, trained office and client personnel in accounting and computer systems. Selected and customized software to meet client needs.

EDUCATION

Pomona Community College, Bachelor's Degree, Business Administration, 1992

That personal touch is evident in this resume—but fortunately, this option is available even to those with less-than-perfect handwriting. The headlines are set in handwriting fonts— you can probably pick up a disk that offers dozens of attractive, printable faces for less than $20.

Jane Smith
123 Main St.
Mytown, State 00000
111/000-0000

Professional Profile

A skilled, seasoned professional with expertise in ...

Inventory auditing
Operational auditing
Financial reporting and administration
Information management and analysis
Web site design

I am energetic, extremely proud of my work, and happy to travel when the need arises.

Systems Knowledge

Extensive experience in Lotus 1-2-3, Excel, Word, PowerPoint, FoxPro, Access, All Clear, Clear Process and Microsoft Operating Systems (including networks).

Education

University of Central Missouri, Brentwood, MO
BA - Accounting, 1995
Posted a 3.55/4.0 GPA.
I completed my degree in three years.

CPA Candidate - sat for the exam in June 1997; results expected October 1997.

Work Experience

Marywell Tool and Die, Kansas City, MO (1996 - present)
Internal Auditor

Engaged in operational auditing at branches throughout the United States. Responsible for inventory auditing, including observations, test counts, and reconciliations on a monthly basis. **Praised as "most reliable member of the department" during face-to-face evaluation, 1996.**

Web Solutions, St. Louis, MO (1995 - 1996)
Web Site Designer

Internet presence provider, advertising real property and high ticket personal property. **Followup research with customers determined that sales leads arising from my sites generated $2.6 million in revenue for company's clients in FY 1996.**

Affiliations and Volunteer Work

Member of the Institute of Internal Auditors
Volunteer—Bradley Street Homeless Shelter

"The best is yet to be!"

This resume makes use of a simple graphic device that carries a wealth of positive associations for potential employers. If you decide to follow this example, use the opportunity to emphasize your own development of "key" solutions!

Jane Smith
123 Main St.
Mytown, State 00000
111/000-0000

EXPERIENCE IS THE KEY TO INCREASED PROFITABILITY FOR ABC CORPORATION.

I am a seasoned professional with extensive experience in global and domestic expansion eager to make a contribution to an aggressively growth-oriented firm.

Experience:

☞ Churn Management Specialist

Singapore First Financial (1993-1995)

Took part in the development and implementation of the company's "top customer" maintenance campaign.

- Adaptable to new situations after being the only foreigner in a large Singapore company.
- Acquired extensive knowledge of customer care and marketing issues while working in the company's churn management team.

☞ **Ranked as #7 performer within 123-person department.**

Administrator
BankLondon (England) (1992-1993)

Learned bank operations and international currency issues as a bank administrator in the world's foremost eurocurrency center.

- Acquired interpersonal and leadership skills through interactions with co-workers of various European cultures.
- Strengthened analytical skills in risk assessment.
- Developed background in global banking issues from analyzing reconcilements and assisting in annual performance analyses.
- Conducted financial projections and forecasts.

☞ **Profiled in English Accountancy's "Ones to Watch" column, January 1993: "Young American on the Move Has International Banking in Her Blood"**

Education:

Bachelor of Science
New York College of Accounting
1992

The approach taken in this resume is probably best reserved for financial firms
with a dynamic, innovative corporate culture.

John Smith
123 Main Street
Mytown, State 00000
111/000-0000

Warning: *Hiring a Less Qualified Mortgage Lending Specialist May Be Hazardous to Your Bottom Line.*

Skill Summary:

Proven management and analytical experience in a financial setting. **Highly skilled** in all major spreadsheet applications; proficient in both Windows and Macintosh computer environments.

Professional Experience:

Pacific Mortgage, Inc., Boise, ID
Mortgage Loan Originator (12/94-Present)

Became third-ranked (out of 45) commission-based employee. Position focused upon mortgage originations through the servicing of real estate professionals in the Boise area. Essential prerequisites for success were: **Competence in FHLMC, FNMA, VA, FHA, RHDC and CHP guidelines**, as well as working knowledge of sub-A lending. A strong emphasis on compliance issues helped me to **find, serve, and maintain new business** effectively.

Mortgage Pro of Boise, Boise, ID
Loan Officer (12/93-12/94)

Originated mortgage-secured loans through servicing of real estate professionals. Program was strictly incentive based. **Named "Employee of the Month" March 1994.**

Western Mortgage, Helena, MT
Managing Broker (12/92-12/93)

Served as Broker of Record for the company within three months. Cited during first personnel review for **"consistently excellent fulfillment of responsibilities in compliance, quality control and lender relations."**

A good example of how a subtle graphic theme can capture attention and interest. The subliminal "rising profits" message is a thoroughly appropriate one, given the nature of the employment inquiry.

Jane Smith
123 Main St.
Mytown, State 00000
111/000-0000

OVERVIEW

A seasoned Financial Services professional seeking expanded opportunities in Securities Sales and Management.

ShareAct (Chicago, IL) 1995-present

Account Executive - Initiated and developed innovative stock reporting division within company; created service design, marketing plan and growth strategy; **expanded service from 1 employee to 5 employees, maintained 100% growth rate, and posted 72% operating profit margin within one year.**

Account Executive - Managed multi-fund solicitations for large mutual funds; developed outbound call strategies based on geographical and numerical profiles of customers. **Ranked consistently in the top four percent of telephone solicitor team.**

Proficient in Lotus 1-2-3, MS Excel, MS Word, MS-DOS, MS Fox-Pro, Windows 95.

Management of multimillion-dollar solicitations, development of proposals to prospective clients, day-to-day management duties. Production of reports for financial analysis. Developed general aptitude in all aspects of business.

I have a Bachelor of Science Degree in Business Administration from Crestmont College (Valley View, IL).

"The only goal you cannot achieve is the one you have not yet recognized." — Stephan Schiffman

The distinctive use of an unconventional heading format sets this resume apart. A few powerful bullets offer highlights from an extensive experience base—and leave the reader wanting to know more.

```
jane smith
123 main street
Mytown, State 00000
111/000-0000
```

career summary:

Seasoned multilingual finance expert, with extensive sales and marketing experience, proven with a track record of successful results. Most recently, served as the Senior Vice President of a multinational natural gas production company.

employment highlights

Fissof: Helsinki, Finland
September 1996-Present

Recruited as the Senior Vice President of Finance for this natural gas production company with facilities in Africa and South America.

Responsible for natural gas sales totaling over $26 million per year, and for managing the company's financial operations.

* Managed budget with cash flow over $28 million, while bringing down cost of production by $2.5 million.

PetroCap Ltd.: Dallas, TX
Capital equipment distributor and engineering services firm active in the petroleum industry.
1993-1996

Recruited as Director of Global Marketing; responsible for strategy and management of the Company's international sales and marketing program. Developed strong international client base for petroleum engineering service and equipment sales. Accomplishments include:

* Successfully concluded contract negotiations on over $90 million of equipment.

United States Air Force
1980-1993

Promoted to progressively responsible positions within the Air Force; my service culminated with my assignment as a Test Officer for a $2.6 billion new system acquisition effort.

* Saved over $4.2 million by locating alternative resources.

education

M.S., Economics, University of Kansas, 1989.

Graduate with honors, Economics, Central Kansas University, 1980.

Fluent in Spanish, Portuguese, and Italian.

Here's a powerful way to accent your experience! As long as they're not overused, bullets like these can be quite effective.

Jane Smith
123 Main Street
Mytown, State 00000
111/000-0000

☞ Personal Profile

Accounting professional with a proven record of achievement as a self- starter with excellent problem-solving skills and superior computer skills. Formal training and working knowledge of Lotus 1-2-3, Microsoft Office, Corel Office Suite, Novell Networks 4.1, Digital UNIX, Microsoft Windows 3.1 and 95, and Foresight MXP manufacturing software.

☞ Education

Little Rock Management College
Little Rock, AR
Associate degree in Accounting, graduated April 1987 with GPA of 3.48. I am currently pursuing a bachelor's degree in Accounting from Cartwright College via evening classes.

☞ Experience

Tobey Technologies, Little Rock, AR
Staff Accountant
11/95 - Present

Responsibilities include:
Tracking and reconciling physical inventory
Developing all written procedures for inventory management and processing
Master scheduling
Revision of corporate standard costing basis
I assisted in the complete overhaul of our network, including employee training, systems, configuration, and administration, resulting in substantial cost savings to our organization.

Little Rock Parks & Recreation Department, Little Rock, AR
Staff Accountant
1992 - 1995

Personally responsible for all accounting activities.
Executed all reports and summaries for senior management.
Processed accounts receivable and accounts payable with high levels of timeliness and accuracy.
Praised for "superior work ethic" by park administrator.

Reflections, Inc., Little Rock, AR
Staff Accountant
1990 - 1993

Personally responsible for all accounts payable functions through general ledger.

Maintained sound inventory control and tracking mechanisms.

Developed daily and weekly cash flow analyses for corporate offices.

Served as informal tech support specialist for users of all office PC software; developed original spreadsheet templates and macros for use in all departments, with significant increases in operational efficiency resulting.

Developed extensive expertise in Lotus 1-2-3.

I was the recipient of the President's Award in 1992 for the best new cost-cutting idea.

SUPERVISOR, FINANCIAL REPORTING

An innovative technique for highlighting key text. By means of an extremely simple graphic device, two dramatic endorsements become even more compelling—and help the author outdistance the competition.

Jane Smith
123 Main St.
Mytown, State 00000
111/000-0000

EXECUTIVE SUMMARY:
An accomplished CPA with a proven track record in…

financial reporting
management of system development
budgeting
accounting
tax operations

Vermont Credit Corporation
Supervisor, Financial Reporting, 1988 - 1996
Accounting Supervisor, 1984 - 1988
Assistant Supervisor, 1980 - 1984

Directed all accounting, budgeting, financial reporting, and tax operations for this national asset-based finance company with portfolios of commercial equipment loans and leases as well as automotive loans and leases ➔ **totaling over $1.6 billion.**

Joined the company at start-up, designing the chart of accounts and writing customized general ledger and financial reporting systems. These programs provided the company with customized and flexible interactive accounting software ➔ **with zero fiscal year expenditure for purchase or licensing fees.**

Developed control systems for retail installment contracts, wholesale dealer financings, private label consumer finance receivables, and tax-oriented leases, facilitating reconciliation and enhancing confidence in the company's financial statements. ➔ **The systems I developed in these areas were in place for the rest of the company's lifetime, until its recent acquisition by BGE International.**

Designed numerous spreadsheet applications, including pricing and profitability model to determine optimal match-funding strategy and to project interest margin for highly leveraged loans and finance leases, based on payment amortization, interest yield curves, and deferred tax parameters. This model enabled the company marketing representatives to quickly understand the true profitability of proposed deals. ➔ **The President of our firm referred to my checklists in this area as "our goofproof prelaunch procedure."**

Led in-house training sessions in basic accounting theory and financial statement analysis for employees in systems, customer service, and credit departments. ➔ **One of my students wrote me a note praising her training period as "the most helpful and instructive I've ever encountered."**

EDUCATION:
BS, Business Administration, 1979
Bellingham University
Wichita, KS

TRUST OFFICER

Wouldn't *you* take a second look at this resume? The unorthodox text formatting serves to emphasize a powerful, direct appeal based on significant potential benefits to the employer. The guarantee near the bottom dramatically addresses any perceived technical shortcomings.

Jane Smith
123 Main St.
Mytown, State 00000
111/000-0000

My motto:
"There is nothing worth doing that is not worth doing right."

EDUCATION

COX UNIVERSITY * San Rafael, CA *
Bachelor of Science, Economics, May 1990

I completed my degree in three years, instead of the standard four. Cumulative GPA 3.6/4.0
I served as Business Manager for the Cox Observer, a popular student newspaper, 1988-1990.

PROFESSIONAL EXPERIENCE

USBANK San Diego, CA *Trust Officer, June 1993-present *

Established and maintained corporate trust and employee benefit packages. Accounts included 16 Fortune 500 corporations. **I have received "excellent" or "outstanding" ratings on my evaluations during every period of my employment at USBANK.**

WEAN HOUSELAND INVESTMENTS * Freedonia, FL * Account Representative, 1990-1993
Supervised from 12-35 employees. Stockbroker for individual and corporate clients. * **Wean Houseland recruited me during my senior year. I was named "Rookie of the Year" after six months.**

COMPUTER EXPERIENCE

MY GUARANTEE: If a software package operates in a Windows or Macintosh environment, and has to do with spreadsheets, word processing, or data management, I can either already use it proficiently or develop a position of expertise within 5 working days.

COMMUNITY ACTIVITIES

GOODWILL INDUSTRIES ANNUAL GAMES
San Rafael, CA Volunteer Coordinator and Referee, 1993, 1994, 1995. **In addition, I installed and customized database and accounting software for the local Goodwill chapter.**

7

Resumes That Quietly Overcome Obstacles

Emphasize Your Strong Suits

The road to valor is built by adversity.
OVID

Who says you can't turn a (perceived) weakness into a strength? Here are some ideas for making compelling, and accurate, statements with your resume, even if you've got a preconceived notion or two to overcome.

This resume highlights the strong suits of an applicant eager to avoid being pigeonholed as a "data entry professional." Note the inclusion of relevant supervisory experience.

John Smith
123 Main Street
Mytown, State 00000
111/000-0000

Will Make a Great Accounting Clerk for ABC Corporation, Thanks to His Superior Performance In...

Accounting (Accounts Receivable, Accounts Payable, Payroll)

Business Math (Including Forecasting)

Information Management (Including Complex Spreadsheet and Word Processing Applications)

Experience

Betty's Bookkeeping
1993 - Present

Maintain sensitive tax-related information on computer database.

File all appropriate tax forms in a timely and accurate manner.

Won "Employee of the Month" award eleven times.

Birmingham Carpentry
Secretary
8/92 - 9/93

Posted financial information both manually and via computer.

Processed daily work orders.

Maintained and updated customer database.

Personally responsible for preliminary work relevant to regular bank and federal deposits.

Cited as "superior performer" in 1992 personnel review.

Birmingham Business School
Part-time Receptionist
11/90 - 7/91

Performed general office duties (answering telephone, taking messages, greeting clients, typing letters, etc.).

Maintained and updated sensitive data on Microsoft Access program.

Verified information provided by new applicants to the school.

Assisted in monthly tabulation of call expenses for tracking purposes; campaign to contain phone costs resulted in 17% reductions in billed totals after only 90 days.

This was a work-study job that helped to defray college expenses.

> *"Cool under Fire"*
>
> During a four-week period in June of 1991, my supervisor was away on sick leave and I was given the responsibilities of Management Information Systems Clerk; I was cited, in a written letter of recommendation arising from this assignment, as "cool under fire, consistently on-target, and a provider of excellent service."

Education

Birmingham Business School 7/95 - 7/96
Clerical Training, Birmingham, AL

This resume handsomely emphasizes management abilities and experience for an opening requiring supervisory expertise and a focus on efficiency.

John Smith
123 Main Street
Mytown, State 00000
111/000-0000

Objective

Seeking to make a contribution to a growing company that will benefit from my administrative, accounting and computer skills and my 14 years of hands-on, results-driven experience with people. Over that period of time, I've ...

* hired, fired and effectively managed employees.
* installed and implemented software to bring dramatic increases in efficiency to offices.
* processed highly sensitive data, including personnel files and proprietary/confidential financial materials.

Watchwork Associates (Hartford, CT)
Accounting Manager
November 1994 - June 1997

Installed and customized AtlantaWay accounting software.
Process payroll, maintain personnel records, interview job candidates,
review employees, manage staff and enforce policies and procedures.
Accurately process accounts payable, accounts receivable, bank
reconciliation; develop a wide variety of financial reports for senior management.
Personally responsible for coordinating and troubleshooting network computer system; authorize purchase of equipment and software, and develop training materials and programs.

Any Time Temps/Temporary Service Agency (Quincy City, MO)
March 1994 - October 1994

* Archer, Rice, & Combs - Data entry and expense report processing.
* Compass Prime Properties - Served as Administrative Assistant to Property Manager; praised as "a superior team player and key contributor at a critical point in time."
* Quincy City Times - Handled circulation data entry work quickly and accurately.

MasterMap, Inc. (St. Louis, MO)
April 1992 - February 1993

* Oversaw office automation campaign; responsible for installation and implementation of accounting, word processing and database applications. Streamlined, revised, and developed office procedures. Processed payroll and maintained sensitive personnel records.

Skills

Excellent PC skills including: Internet, AtlantaWay III, Word, Excel, Lotus.

ACCOUNTING PROFESSIONAL

No degree yet—and your most recent employment is not directly relevant to the position for which you're applying. Here's one strategy for shining anyway—note the innovative use of the footnote!

Jane Smith
123 Main Street
Mytown, State 00000
111/000-0000

A talented, creative team player eager to deliver results for ABC Company.

Experience

Moriarty & Associates, Legal Accounting Department
July 1991 to August 1994*

Position: Trust & Estate Accounting Clerk

Personally responsible for preparation of schedules of gains, losses, disbursements and income receipts on each asset. Investigated information for asset verification and researched prior activity in accounts. Calculated terminating commissions and completed income accrual for trust accounting. Most of my work was done on a Porex/Fiduciary Accounting System and Master-Pro computers with WordMaster software. Supervisor said he "hated to see me go" when time came for me to relocate to another town due to spouse's transfer.

Bay State Utility Services, Inc.
May 1990 to July 1991

Position: Accounting Assistant (Internship)

Quickly mastered Wang microcomputer system. Prepared billing statements; adjusted, balanced and reconciled accounting records for private utility companies and over thirty regional affiliate organizations. Performed filing and organizational tasks; posted cash on a daily basis.

Education

Bay State University, Milton, MA. Major: Accounting.
Expected date of graduation: August 1998 (Part-time student)
Connecticut Institute of Technology, Hartford, CT. Completed 40 quarter-credit hours in bachelor's degree program. Major: Accounting.

* Since 1994 I have been active at home, bringing up our two children and occasionally taking on non-accounting-related temporary assignments through JB Personnel (Peabody, MA). I have received consistently excellent evaluations from clients for my word processing and database management work during this period; photocopies of these are available for your review.

Here's a resume that emphasizes hands-on experience to overcome the potential problems inherent in the lack of a formal degree. Note the Independent Consultant entry at
the top—a convenient and, as used here, completely legitimate way to account for time
spent outside the formal 9-5 employment world. The use of a quotation at the end of the
resume is striking and effective.

Jane Smith
123 Main St.
Mytown, State 00000
111/000-0000

WORK EXPERIENCE

August 1995-Present:
Jane Smith Associates

Accounting Specialist (Independent Consultant)
Contract personal financial management services to help individuals and organizations operate at maximum efficiency.

Set up computerized accounting systems and train end users in a wide variety of
businesses; each system I install is **customized to the needs of the organization.**

Complete accurate tax returns for individuals and businesses.

Handle accounting work related to **estates and wills** for area attorneys.

Execute periodic **time-sensitive accounting work (such as year-end closing and
yearly and monthly financial reports)** to a high degree of accuracy.

Client contacts (and personal references) include:
James Welton, North Shore Animal Rights League (508/555-1213)
Ellen Kruse, Squaniak Bay Elder Care Center (508/555-1214)
Martin Shilway, Arrowhead Business Services (508/555-1215)

1993-1995:
Reading Is Essential (Breen, NC)

Financial Officer
Personally responsible for all financial affairs of this local nonprofit organization
(banking, payroll, financial statements, books of original entry).

Met all deadlines in **accurately filing all state and federally mandated reports.**

Served as Assistant Manager in Manager's absence. Resolved sensitive personnel
matters, interpreted and enforced policies, and acted as provisional Recording Secretary to
the Board of Directors during regularly scheduled Board meetings.

1992-1993:
Emeryville College of Technology (Emeryville, NC)

Contract Instructor (Accounting and Finance)
Instructed students in business plan writing and presentation. **Taught Principles of Accounting course** to Advanced Business Operations students.

1983-1991:
Fishkill Industries (Fishkill, NY)

Accountant - Front Line Supervisor
Supervised between eight and twelve employees; reported to Head of Divisional Accounting. Personally responsible for operation of capital accounting system. Developed and implemented customized computerized accounting systems that resulted in **significant improvements in accuracy and efficiency.**

Developed **timely, accurate consolidated financial statements** for the Northeast Division.

Member in good standing, Certified General Accountants Association.

"A love of delay generally breeds danger." — Miguel de Cervantes

ACCOUNTING SUPERVISOR

An accounting supervisor with ample experience in the for-profit sector who wants to move into the nonprofit world for the first time. Note the emphasis on "mission," an important concept within the target company.

Jane Smith
123 Main St.
Mytown, State 00000
111/000-0000

KEY TRAITS FOR SUCCESS AT KREW-TV, MARYLAND PUBLIC BROADCASTING

A demonstrated record of achievement as an accounting supervisor.

A sense of mission.

A commitment to the timely, accurate fulfillment of departmental goals.

Professional Experience

As Accounting Manager for Acme Property Management (September 1996-present):

* Responsible for accounts receivable, accounts payable, bank reconciliation, general ledger, financial statements, and statement of cash flows for 12 properties.

* Projected revenues, expenses, and cash needs for the purpose of funding and budgeting.

* Converted accruals to cash basis for reporting to banks and the Resolution Trust Corporation.

* Improved timeliness and accuracy of financial reports by revising month-end procedures.

* Implemented conversion of properties to new accounting system.

* Received Great Idea of the Quarter award and company recognition for developing and implementing a debit balance collection procedure that resulted in company savings of over $30,000 during a 3-month time period.

As an Inventory Accounting Specialist for Wheeling Manufacturing (January 1995-August 1996):

* Made periodic trips to facilities in Guatemala and Costa Rica to monitor accounting systems and suggest review.

* Maintained perpetual inventory system for multiple warehouses.

* Integrated accounts payable system into daily operation.

* Prepared general ledger account reconciliations, cost of goods manufactured, cost of goods sold, and customer profit reports.

* Analyzed raw material variances utilizing standard cost system and bills of material.

* Responsible for month-end procedures for the purchase order, inventory, and accounts payable modules.

* Prepared and presented data for external auditors.

As an Accounting Supervisor for Wheeling Manufacturing (July 1993-January 1995):

*   Supervised accounts payable staff.

*   Processed manual accounts payable reconciliations to the general ledger.

*   Prepared general ledger account reconciliations.

*   Processed employee expense reports and reconciled employee travel advance accounts.

*   Responsible for month-end closing for accounts payable system.

I was praised as "a key contributor with a real sense of mission" in my most recent personnel review.

Education

August 1989 - May 1993
Colorado State University
Degree: BS in Sociology
I was employed on a full-time basis for most of my college years in order to subsidize my education.
GPA: 3.65

Skilled in: Lotus 1-2-3 v. 5, Excel 6.0, QuattroPro 5.0, WordPerfect 6.0, Microsoft Word 6.0, Windows 95 and 3.1, Internet software for World Wide Web.

Member, Rocky Mountain Accounting Society

Member, Guild of Management Accountants

Member, American Inventory Control and Manufacturing Oversight Society

A sterling example of a resume designed to take the pressure off an employer—a good strategy for those situations when you don't know whether a formal opening exists yet. Remember: A considerable portion of those hired on as temporary workers eventually receive offers of full-time employment.

Jane Smith
123 Main St.
Mytown, State 00000
111/000-0000

HOW LONG? THAT'S UP TO YOU.

My objective is to perform exceptionally high-quality audit and/or accounting services on a contract or permanent basis for any period, short or long.

EXPERIENCE: In-depth experience in all areas of auditing and financial accounting, including management and implementing accounting systems

I have worked in many settings over the years:

Reconciliations and analysis, with emphasis on spreadsheet applications
Credit and collections
Controller
Internal audit
Corporate accounting
Public accounting
Owned a small crosstown courier business

EDUCATION:

MBA, Accounting, Berrigan University, Johnstown, PA
BFA, Mellingham University, Memphis, TN
CPA Exam (Passed first time.)

Employers/clients include...

AccountWorks (temporary service)
ABC Materials (during acquisition by GenCo)
American Mortgage
Troubador Transportation
Americar
WHHY (Public Television affiliate for Corwin, PA)
Vera Transportation
Quickee Delivery (I was a franchisee.)

DETAILED EMPLOYMENT HISTORY:

COURIER EXPRESS
1996-Present Johnstown, PA
Data Conversion Operator (Part-Time)

ACCOUNTWORKS
1994-1996 Johnstown, PA
Performed accounting duties at various client companies in the Johnstown area on temporary as-signments. **As a result of one temporary assignment, I was named Accounting Manager** at the Corporate Office of ABC Materials during its acquisition by Genco in the fall of 1995, a position I held for four months before returning to short-term assignments through AccountWorks.

QUICKEE DELIVERY
1992-1994 Johnstown, PA
Owned a franchise within this national delivery chain.

VERA TRANSPORTATION
1987-1992 Pittsburgh, PA
A national trucking company.
Responsible for accounting, financial analysis, and credit/collection for this company and its sub-sidiaries.

TROUBADOR TRANSPORTATION
1976-1987 Newark, NJ
Regional Controller, Eastern Region
1986-1987
Directed all accounting activities for operations in the eastern U.S. and Puerto Rico.

Manager, Corporate Accounting 1983-1986
Responsible for corporate consolidations, annual report, SEC reporting
and accounting for parent company.

Supply Division Controller 1980-1983
Responsible for accounting, financial analysis, and credit analysis for
the division. Division sold transportation-related products and
services, and performed the purchasing function for the Corporation.

Internal Auditing Specialist 1976-1980
Began as a Senior Auditor and was promoted to Supervisor. Responsible for supervising and completing audits of subsidiaries and making recommendations for improvement.

"Work does not leave my hands unless I am prepared to put my name to it."

BENEFITS ADMINISTRATOR

This applicant wants to move from a sales environment to a benefits administration
setting. The challenge: to emphasize adaptability and make the very most of existing skills.
The headline—and indeed the whole of the resume—is highly targeted toward a
single employer.

Jane Smith
123 Main Street
Mytown, State 00000
111/000-0000

Education

Charlotte College, Charlotte, NC
B.S., Financial Planning (1993)

I am a dynamic, high-achievement team player who wants to make a significant contribution to the Benefits Department of ABC Corporation.

Experience

Ready Investments /Investment Specialist (Charlotte, NC)
Aug. 1996 - Dec. 1997

*   Developed and marketed a wide variety of successful retirement products.

*   Developed in-depth knowledge of financial portfolio issues.

*   Conducted seminars on life insurance selection.

*   Trained and motivated over 200 employees in dealing with customer questions concerning Ready products.

Stanley Insurance /Agent (Charlotte, NC)
1994-1996

*   Developed proposals in life insurance and health needs.

*   Implemented insurance and health packages for groups and individuals.

*   Cited for "excellence in client service" (personnel evaluation, 1996).

*   One of Stanley's top 25 rookies nationwide in 1994.

Dade County Boy's Club /Athletic Director (Miami, FL)
1986-1993

*   Developed and implemented athletic programs; responsibilities included planning, budgets, travel and special events.

*   Coordinated all staff scheduling.

*   Co-chair of all committees in the program.

*   Personally responsible for the recruiting and motivation of staff and members.

*   Served as liaison with state regulatory officials.

Here's a resume that makes the most of a pertinent community college degree, rather than the bachelor's degree the employer may expect. The inclusion of grade point averages is a plus—as long as the grades you're citing are over 3.0!

Jane Smith
123 Main St.
Mytown, State 00000
111/000-0000

My goal is to obtain a position within the Oakland, California area that will challenge me professionally and take full advantage of what a former supervisor called my "boundless energy and significant experience" within the accounting field.

PROFESSIONAL EXPERIENCE

Freedom Mortgage, Inc.
San Francisco, CA (6/94 - 6/97)

Construction Loan Accountant/Credit Analyst

* Updated and administered creditworthiness guidelines for evaluation of new loan applications.
* Managed $215,000 loan program with minimal supervision.
* Provided customer service to branch offices nationwide.
* Reconciled general ledger accounts and prepared monthly reports for management.

Freedom Card Services
South San Francisco, CA (3/94 - 6-94)

Front-Line Credit Analyst

* Determined the creditworthiness of applicants.
* Handled daily requests and complaints of customers.
* Promoted to Construction Loan Accountant after three months as a result of "superior" performance.

Doborski Engineering, Inc.
Oakland, CA (3/93 - 8/93)

Accounting Clerk / Summer Internship

* Assisted independent auditors with annual audit.
* Responsible for daily cash deposits, typically in excess of $60,000.
* Organized and maintained accounts payable files.

Vererri Bookkeeping & Tax Service
Oakland, California (11/92 - 3/83)

Bookkeeper

* Drafted accurate individual tax returns for review.
* Performed various accounting services for several small business clients.
* Prepared and managed payroll for clients, including preparation of quarterly tax returns.

EDUCATION AND RELEVANT TRAINING/EXPERIENCE

Associate's Degree, May 1992
Bersami College, Petaluma, CA
Accounting and Education
3.69 GPA (Cum Laude)

Expert in the operation of:

* Lotus 1-2-3
* Microsoft Excel
* Microsoft Access
* PowerPoint
* Word for Windows
* Windows 95

CUSTOMER ACCOUNT REPRESENTATIVE (COLLECTIONS)

Sometimes, having held a higher-than-average number of jobs in the field means you should consider providing just enough information to get you in the door. Here's an example of a resume that manages this task nicely.

Jane Smith
123 Main St.
Mytown, State 00000
111/000-0000

Management/Supervision Experience:

* Four years of high performance in a Customer Service/Collection staff supervision/management environment.
* Personally responsible for departmental budgeting and cost control.
* Reduction of bad debt in my department was cited as a **"breakthrough accomplishment"** in company newsletter (March 1995).

Training Experience:

Oversaw selection of outside consultants to conduct in-house seminars on topics selected by the President of my company; **praised as someone who "knows how to pick great programs" by top management during my annual performance review.**

Personally responsible for individual and group training in customer service and collection areas; **fourteen of the twenty people who reported to me for training were promoted within twelve months.**

Handled negotiation of contractual agreements between employer and outside vendors; **my contract evaluation guidelines were adopted companywide.**

Software and Computer Skills:

Proficient with advanced spreadsheet programming and multiple word processor packages. **I am highly skilled in MS Excel, Lotus 1-2-3, Microsoft Word, and WordPerfect, and fluent in many other environments.**

Analyzed current in-house and outside agency systems for system development and improvement. **My evaluation of preliminary program led to key improvements in our customized Management Information package.**

Professional and Educational Summary (1994-present):

American Central Finance (current employer)
Collections Associate
Supervisor of Collections

VeraCruz Financial
Collections Associate

Radio Research Corporation
Inside Sales Representative

Boston Computer Museum
Accounting/Information Services Intern

I graduated with honors from Central Plains High School (1986) and received an associate Degree in Business Services from Montclair Community College (1990).

"There are no boundaries save those imposed by the human mind."
    — Helen Brantwell (British essayist)

FINANCIAL ANALYST

An excellent resume for a parent reentering the workforce. Given the circumstances, the omission of dates is probably justified—but be ready to supply all the details during an interview! Note: Many employers are extremely suspicious of unexplained employment gaps of more than six months.

Jane Smith
123 Main St.
Mytown, State 00000
111/000-0000

Since 1995, I have worked at home full-time raising my youngest daughter Tracy, who is now ready to spend the hours between 7:30 a.m. and 5:30 p.m. in a different setting. So am I!

Deveen Communications (1994-1995)
Part-time Assistant to the Senior Vice President of Finance.

Responsible for preparing corporate operating budgets, fixed-asset depreciation, reconciling subsidiary ledgers, preparing property tax returns, and compiling federal tax return work-papers. **Referred to as "indispensable" by Senior Vice President of Finance.**

Beacon Page
Accounting Manager.

Managed a centralized billing (A/R) operation for this telecommunications company. Developed updated management reports for accounts receivable, sales, and inventory analysis.

PhoneWorks (1992-1994)
Plant Manager.

Oversaw project planning, production scheduling, software development, application engineering, and servicing of various PhoneWorks internal systems. Responsible for materials and capacity planning and facility allocation in four different work groups. Prepared and analyzed forecasting models for optimizing/minimizing standard cost variances. **Implemented cost reduction processes while improving throughput by 150%.**

Assisted the Corporate and Regulatory Accounting wings of the company with the compilation of financial statements for regulators. **Developed budget models and forecasting tools using computer financial simulation on BeRight software.**

TaxMate Service (Part-time work, 1989-1991)
Income Tax Service Company
Executive Tax Preparer.

Consulted with clients to formulate the **most beneficial legal tax returns for individuals and small businesses.** Researched and applied the Internal Revenue Code and Tax Rulings appropriately for filing of federal tax returns.

Education

Vanson State University - Bachelor of Science Degree in Accounting, 1989

Community Involvement

Internal Revenue Service - (VITA) Volunteer Income Tax Assistance

Prepared federal tax returns for individuals, sole proprietors and small businesses in the local community. **(Regular volunteer since leaving the workforce.)**

References

John Varison, PhoneWorks (617/555-1212)

Mel Powers, TaxMate (413/555-1212)

FINANCIAL ANALYST

An excellent example of a resume that wins attention and interest for the applicant—despite his lack of previous professional experience within the field.

John Smith
123 Main St.
Mytown, State 00000
111/000-0000

My professional mission is to deliver measurable increases in departmental performance as a full-time financial analyst to a leading financial services firm such as ABC Corporation.

PERSONAL PROFILE

MBA, Finance (3.85 GPA), Massachusetts Tech University, Worcester, MA, May 1998
* Dean's List (Finance)
* International Education Scholarships
* Research and Teaching Assistantships
* National Dean's List Scholarship Finalist (Top 60 in U.S.)
* Beta Gamma Sigma Business Society

BS, Business Administration (3.83 GPA), Powers University, Cumberland, RI, May 1996
* Area of Business Scholarship (Top Student)
* Valedictorian
* Powers Public Speaking Club (2 years)
* Intramural sports: baseball, volleyball, soccer

FINANCE-RELATED EXPERIENCE

Executive Director
Student Direct Fund, Powers University
January 1996 - May 1996

* Oversaw and reviewed all accounting transactions.
* Personally executed all fund security transactions. Personally maintained all non-accounting records and archived documents received. Monitored physical facilities assigned to the fund, and engaged in computer-related troubleshooting.

Research Assistant: Minority Entrepreneurship Project

* Served as Research Assistant on Professor Melvin DeWitt's landmark 1996 paper in *Minority Entrepreneurship* on bankruptcy patterns in inner-city neighborhoods, and was praised in that paper for my "thorough, reliable, and accurate analyses of complex economic situations."

COMPUTER SKILLS

* Familiar with Lotus 1-2-3, Microsoft Office, and other standard business software.

The author of this resume is seeking to make a transition from contract work to a full-time position. Note the emphasis on project management skills.

Jane Smith
123 Main St.
Mytown, State 00000
111/000-0000

"Jane brings superior project management skills to the fore,
day in and day out, week in and week out."
— Ellen Berrigan, JBG/DocCo Corporation

PROFESSIONAL EXPERIENCE

Contract Programmer/Analyst, JBG/DocCo, Elmira, NY, 10/94 to present.

MarketContact project: Reengineered global business processes covering all phases of customer relationships, including marketing products, developing sales solutions, and managing customer contracts. Investigated current system and analyzed proposed future state processes. Formulated and documented technical solutions, and coordinated design with others to ensure consistency across functional groups.

CommissionPro project: Designed and implemented major enhancements for DocCo's commission payment system for sales agents. Performed analysis and code changes for SellTime, the subsystem used by agents to develop contract worksheets, create orders and contract proposals, and keep track of available products, prices, and financing options. Oversaw creation and modification of all queries, forms, and procedures.

Participated in DocCo "Accelerated Leadership" training program, June 1996.

Staff Consultant, Triple A Consulting, Hartford, CT, 1/91 to 2/93.

Projects included installations at two major utility companies and an information plan for a major area hospital. Responsibilities included supervision of programmers, design and programming of custom modules, and analysis and documentation of object-oriented information flow.

Other work experience includes general ledger, payroll, customer service, fund raising, and retail.

COMPUTER SKILLS

Microsoft Office, Lotus 1-2-3, Lotus Notes, MultiMate AdvantageII, WordPerfect, WordStar, Lotus Symphony, Harvard Graphics

EDUCATION

M.S. in Economics, December 1997, The University of Montana, Helena, MT (night classes).

B.S. in Economics, May 1992, The University of Montana, Helena, MT
Concentration in Finance. Graduated Summa Cum Laude in Honors Program.

INTERNAL AUDITOR/ACCOUNTING MANAGER

Lots of experience in a variety of areas? Remember that you must pick and choose creatively. Your resume is an ad, not a transcript of legal testimony. Here's a model that shows one way to highlight only what is relevant to the position in question.

Jane Smith
123 Main St.
Mytown, State 00000
111/000-0000

SUMMARY: An experienced executive with deep financial experience and a proven ability to manage small- and medium-sized companies. Skilled at anticipating problems and setting up practical, timely and cost-effective solutions. Cost-conscious, innovative, resourceful and entrepreneurial. Creative, detail oriented professional with strong communication skills, budgeting, cash management, operations and financial analysis experience. Familiar with popular computer software environments, including Microsoft office, Lotus 1-2-3, and ACT!

CAREER HIGHLIGHTS:

ACCOUNTING

* Launched a new accounting department, including staff recruitment and training and operating procedures implementation. **Established all-new set of internal controls that saved $114,000.**

* Established new spreadsheet format to compare financial ratios for nine divisions and consolidated statements for senior management. **My reporting formats were praised as "excellent" by the president of the company.**

* Directed all accounting functions including **payables, receivables, fixed assets, cash management, general ledger, inventory and payroll.**

* Set up comprehensive system for planning, conducting, and reporting results of a $13.5 million physical inventory, **reducing inventory variance to less than .002%.**

AUDITING

* Headed audit team that established prudent credit procedures for defective and returnable products; **these standards resulted in the recovery of $1,754,000.**

* Audited 1400 transactions in an acknowledged check-kiting scheme and **documented 187 instances, with a total value in excess of $11,000,000.**

* Audited a county fixed-asset system and established existence of many unauthorized expenses; **resulting new procedures led to cost savings of $1,425,000.**

MANAGEMENT

* Established **effective policies and procedures** for personnel, purchasing, and facilities management.

* As Safety Director, devised and implemented a thorough Illness & Injury Prevention Program that was **in full compliance with OSHA guidelines.**

* Developed quantifiable clerical and technical performance standards that **resulted in annual savings of $600,000.**

ADMINISTRATION

* Established a self-insured medical/dental program which resulted in **reduced absenteeism and savings of $322,000.**

* Oversaw all aspects of a global corporation insurance program investing **$4,000 for specific coverage resulting in a $116,000 payoff due to the covered loss.**

* Set up supply purchasing program for non-capital items that resulted in **cost reductions of 36%.**

ACCOUNTING EXPERIENCE:

Internal Auditor, Essex County, MA

Tax Accountant, K&S Personnel (Temporary Assignments), Danvers, MA

Accounting Manager, Leisure International, Boston, MA

Accountant/Consultant, Tirando & Co., Certified Public Accountants, Austin, TX

General Accounting Manager, Merton Technologies, Dallas, TX

EDUCATION:

B.S. Business Administration, Finance/Insurance, University of Texas at Ft. Worth

INVENTORY CONTROLLER

Here, the lack of a formal degree is more than compensated for by a host of excellent references and ample hands-on experience. The opening line lets the reader know a seasoned professional has entered the building.

Jane Smith
123 Main St.
Mytown, State 00000
111/000-0000

A tested Inventory Control Specialist with the ability to make an immediate contribution to your organization's bottom line.

Summary

* I have held inventory control related positions in various retail marketing settings including construction materials and auto sales. I am experienced in inventory control in both areas. I have a strong "natural number sense" and deep interpersonal sales and customer service experience.

Typically, my work has required scheduling and coordinating the delivery and estimating of building materials to contractors and retail customers. I pride myself on **accuracy, accountability, and practical problem solving.**

Work Experience

Mel's Contracting, Eastville, OH 11-91 to present
Office Manager/Estimator

* Provided inventory control and support for this independent contracting operation for the past four years. Assisted in providing accurate estimates to expanding base of customers. Knowledgeable about all phases of the (residential) construction business. **Hold final responsibility for all materials acquisition and inventory management tasks.**

Brewster Volvo, Brewster, OH 1-86 to 10-91
Assistant Parts Manager (promoted to) Inventory Controller

* Responsible for the supply and levels control of auto parts and accessories within thriving dealership and to retail customers. **Responsible for all aspects of inventory control and employee scheduling for a staff of six associates.**

Rick's Lumber Co., Mica, CA 12-84 to 12-85
Inventory Controller/Contractor Coordinator/Sales Associate

* Responsible for the weekly and monthly reporting of material usage and levels and the ordering and resupplying of building materials/hardware. **Provided accurate sales and materials estimates for customers.**

References

Steve Newton, Rick's Lumber, 123 Border Street, Mica, CA (818/555-1212)

Kirby Denson, Editor, Eastville News, Eastville, OH (303/555-1212)

INVESTMENT/SYSTEMS ACCOUNTANT

No academic degree—and an unorthodox point of entry to a financial career. This resume uses a key endorsement to put the emphasis where it ought to be—on tangible accomplishments within the field.

Jane Smith
123 Main St.
Mytown, State 00000
111/000-0000

PROFILE: An experienced Investment/Systems Accountant with an extensive computerized accounting background.

CAREER HIGHLIGHTS

Had an essential role in the changeover from a mainframe accounting system to a PC based system. Regional manager on my performance: **"We couldn't have done it without you."**

As a result of deep experience with software packages such as Lotus 1-2-3 and WordPerfect, I have been able to **streamline and automate many routine duties** through the development of macros and cross-program "fixes."

Specialize in the identification and **permanent resolution of information-management accounting problems,** thanks to extensive knowledge of Excel, Lotus 1-2-3, and OS/2 v2.11, OS/2 Warp, as well as DOS 6.22, Windows 3.x, and Windows 95.

PROFESSIONAL EXPERIENCE

The Waltham Insurance Group (Waltham, MA)
August 1996 - Present
Investment / Systems Accountant

Personally responsible for the management of the firm's extensive portfolio of long-term and short-term investments, including stocks, bonds and mortgage-backed securities.

* **Develop error-free reporting systems.** Established system for accurately recording and updating transactions for Waltham's $1.6 billion in assets, in both Canadian and US currencies, including calculating currency translation, amortization, capital gains/losses and accruals.

* **Boost cash flow.** Ascertain that income due via bond interest, dividends, etc. is received on correct due dates.

* **Keep up with new developments.** Maintain daily correspondence with five different investment managers concerning portfolio activities.

* **Maintain sound internal reporting.** Execute quarterly and monthly reconciliations of Statement of Securities to sub-ledgers and general ledger.

* **Determine value and income.** Perform accurate calculations of income accruals and market values for quarterly reporting purposes.

August 1992 - August 1996

Started as Reconciliation Clerk; promoted in March 1995 to Investment Associate, and then, in August 1996, to Systems Accountant.

* **Helped to launch new accounting system that resulted in significant costs savings companywide.** Performed comprehensive troubleshooting work in response to problem reports from accounting departments in all branches in New England region. Changed procedures and system configurations to help make new companywide accounting system trouble-free.

* **Supported advanced software applications for new users.** Established user-friendly macros automating the design and layout of ReportWiz reports. (These were used in all offices throughout the New England region.)

* **Offered as-needed technical assistance.** Helped coworkers in solving daily computer-related problems.

* **Made the transition a smooth one.** Helped complete bank reconciliations due to complications arising from changeover from old accounting system to new.

OTHER WORK AND EDUCATIONAL EXPERIENCE

Supreme Sub Shops
Nov. 1987 - June 1992
Food Services Manager

Started with Supreme in 1985 as a delivery person and worked my way up to the position of manager.

A young manager, I took advantage of the opportunity to develop new supervisory skills and combined this with a natural ability to **interact effectively with subordinates of all ages.**

Certified General Accountants Association of Greater Boston
Brookline, MA
Currently enrolled as Level V student.

MANAGER/FINANCIAL ANALYST

The victim of a layoff who has since founded a one-person independent consulting operation wishes to reenter the workforce. As noted elsewhere, the legitimate development of various consulting assignments is an excellent way to account for what might otherwise appear to be ominous gaps in one's employment record.

John Smith
123 Main St.
Mytown, State 00000
111/000-000

SUMMARY:

I am looking for a position in financial management that will take advantage of my four years of financial analysis experience and two years of managerial experience. **My research indicates that ABC Corporation is in an excellent position to benefit from my contributions.**

ASSETS:

Superior computer skills: MS Excel, MS Access, MS Word, and other popular programs.

Proven record of success in budgeting, financial analysis, margin analysis, pricing, and general management.

Excellent analytical and interpersonal skills.

FINANCIAL HISTORY:

AccountPro Systems (1996 - Present)

Assist a wide variety of clients in managing financial reporting and internal controls issues. Praised as a **"committed problem solver who can bring projects in on time and under budget."**

Belt Promotions (Dallas, TX, 1997 - Present)

Provide one-on-one finance-related business consulting services for a wide variety of area businesses. 22 clients served. I serve as President of this financial services firm.

Colspan Corporation (Austin, TX, 1993 - 1996)

Financial Analyst with responsibilities including budgeting, pricing and bid management, financial reporting, financial analysis, outlook/opportunity reporting, and internal controls. In 1996, I was **selected to manage the Accounting Department, and supervised sixteen full-time employees.**

AmeriGrade (Austin, TX, 1989 - 1993)

Accounting Clerk. Oversaw posting of payments, reconciliations, and preparation of important financial reports. **Received five consecutive positive annual evaluations.**

EDUCATION:

BS, Finance and Economics, Jersey City Business College (1993)
MBA: Northeastern Business University (1995)

SEEKING ENTRY-LEVEL POSITION

Here's an example of a dramatic approach that works quite well to highlight strengths that might otherwise be overlooked, due to the candidate's lack of formal work experience. This approach can be quite effective when directed to the right person at the right firm.

Jane Smith
123 Main Street
Mytown, State 00000
111/000-0000

Stop the presses!

#1 student in a demanding accounting class of 525 at the University of Indiana (May 1997); on graduation, I won class honors and was named a Mildred B. Bettelworth Scholar.

Current objective: Find a challenging position as a financial professional within Cooper News Corporation that will allow me to use my creative and analytical abilities to add significant value. I have strong experience with client interviews and sales. In addition to accounting, I have also studied international business, micro and macro economics, and the economics of labor supply.

Work Experience

Applicon, Bloomington, MN (July 1996-present)
Telemarketer

Retrieve client files from computer database.

Contact and survey clients.

Accurately complete computer database forms.

Prepare accurate quotes.

Evaluate individual client needs and respond with potential benefits.

Named top telemarketer in office for August 1996.

Proficient in Microsoft Office.

Education: Bachelor's degree in Business (honors), University of Indiana (1997).

SEEKING ENTRY-LEVEL POSITION

Let's face it. The first job is often the toughest to track down. Here's a compelling arrangement of relevant experience for an applicant seeking his first professional position after graduation.

John Smith
123 Main Street
Mytown, State 00000
111/000-0000

> "A rigorous work ethic is the shrewdest career strategy of all."
> —James Smith (my father)

EDUCATION

Northern California College, Los Angeles
Bachelor's Degree Candidate, August 1998
Major: International Economics

Coursework includes: International Trade and Finance, Public Finance, Managerial Accounting, Money and Banking, Econometrics, C++ and Pascal, Programming, Statistics

EXPERIENCE:

Data Processing Assistant, Sept 97 - June 98
International Studies Department, Northern California College

* Maintained high degrees of promptness and accuracy; selected to oversee training efforts with new team members.

* Set up detailed reports of employees' vacation hours and sick leaves for senior management.

* Customized data output formats for use by Director's office in reorganization campaign.

Receptionist/Administrative Assistant, Sept 1996 - Sept 1997
Financial Aid Office, Northern California College

* Developed extensive knowledge of regulations concerning funds, loans, and related issues.

* Assisted students in resolution of a wide variety of financial aid problems.

Summer Study Abroad Program, Summer 1995
Summer Program to Ukraine, Northern California College

* Symposium Committee member, organized symposium with Ukrainian families.

* Handled initial budgeting, forecasting, and scheduling work.

* With rest of Symposium Committee, concluded trip under allocated budget.

I have an in-depth knowledge of financial and database software in both PC and Macintosh applications.

SEEKING ENTRY-LEVEL POSITION

No professional work background whatsoever! But note the dramatic emphasis on relevant college and volunteer activities. This is far more effective than a dry recitation of grades and objectives.

John Smith
123 Main St.
Mytown, State 00000
111/000-0000

Committed to Excellence in Accounting

SKILLS

Teamwork

* Served as Business Manager on campus newspaper, worked harmoniously with staff writers.
* Raised money for yearly Students in Design competition.
* Helped to organize study groups in three accounting-related classes.
* Collaborated with team to complete community service projects for senior citizens.

Leadership

* Coordinated community service projects (volunteer tax form help) for local senior citizens.
* Organized and scheduled weekly Community Care meetings.
* Helped coordinate academic and social events for student group.

Communication

* Tutored high-school students in basic accounting concepts.
* Wrote weekly articles on business matters for campus newspaper.
* Sold advertisements to businesses and on-campus organizations for campus newspaper.
* Developed Reach Out with Learning program and manuals.
* Presented three projects at the Students in Design competition (one was selected as a finalist).

CAMPUS INVOLVEMENT

Treasurer, Future Management Accountants of Portland University (1996, 1997)
Business Manager, Portland University *Scribe* (student newspaper)
Students in Design, Portland University, Portland, OR 1994-97

EXPERIENCE

Office Intern - Portland University Office of Career Services (Summer 1996)
Camp Counselor - Camps Wahconah and Potomac, Pittsfield, MA (Summer 1994)

HONORS

Sidney Feinstein Scholarship

EDUCATION

Bachelor of Science degree (with honors), concentration in Business Administration, 3.6/4.0 GPA, Portland University, 1997.

This resume overcomes a lack of specific mainframe computer skills sought by the hiring organization by highlighting ample parallel experience.

John Smith
123 Main St.
Mytown, State 00000
111/000-0000

Profile:

I am currently a graduate student at the University of Welfleet. I will obtain a Master's degree in Accounting **within the next thirty days**. On May 12th, 1994, I received a Bachelor of Science degree in Accounting and Management Information Systems from Commonwealth College (**Accounting GPA 3.6; Management Information Systems GPA 3.7).** I am eager to put my **significant experience in accounting and information systems** to work for a global company in search of someone with a **passion for achievement and accuracy in finance-related areas.**

Professional Experience:

Computer Answer Center Assistant, University of Welfleet
Welfleet, MA
June 1995 - August 1995

*   Offer tutoring services in various software applications and in C language programming.
*   **Provide extensive hardware and software support** for UW staff and students.

Intern, Opportunity Consultants, Inc.
Worcester, MA
August 1994 - May 1995

*   **Troubleshot** financial service system computer problems; helped consultants in the configuration and implementation of customized software.
*   **Developed** extensive customized documentation (manuals, quick-start summary sheets, procedure breakdowns) for key clients.
*   **Conducted** exhaustive tests of existing procedures and made recommendations to consultants.
*   **Maintained** on-line Help Library for client intranet use.
*   **Captured** new customers (with full-time consultants) through detailed preliminary research and attendance and support at on-site demonstrations.

Accounting Assistant, SellRight, Inc.
Springfield, MA
August 1993 - August 1994

*   **Maintained** general ledger; praised for "consistently punctual and accurate work."
*   **Prepared** monthly bank reconciliations.
*   **Installed** and updated accounting software; customized to specifications of the Accounting Manager.
*   **Processed** monthly reports for company clients.

Tax Preparer, TaxCo Corporation, Inc.
Cambridge, MA
January 1993 - August 1993

* **Offered accurate tax advice** to consumers during face-to-face meetings.
* **Completed** all necessary entries in a timely manner.
* **Filed** returns electronically via FDW Systems.
* **Provided** overtime assistance during peak periods.

Research Assistant, SellRight, Inc.
Springfield, MA
February 1992 - August 1993

* **Analyzed** stocks and open-ended mutual funds using TeleReport system.
* **Surveyed** opportunities for stock investment in the Pacific Rim; forwarded recommendations that resulted in **$212,000 net gain.**
* **Monitored** Massachusetts-based public firms.

Proficient in a wide variety of software and hardware environments.

An example of a highly customized resume. Note how the applicant—who seeks a position within a prestigious nonprofit foundation—emphasizes volunteer phone work to establish the proper fit. The resume also profiles the applicant's nonprofit-sector clients.

Jane Smith
123 Main St.
Mytown, State 00000
111/000-0000

Personal Profile

By instinct a thorough, reliable, organized, and analytical accounting professional seeking an opportunity to put proven strengths to work for the right nonprofit organization. **Over a quarter-century of demonstrated performance serving clients both in and out of the nonprofit sector.**

PROFESSIONAL EXPERIENCE

1993 to Present:
Morton and Valdez LLC, CPAs (Chicago, IL)

Oversight Manager

Duties include review of audit, review and compilation engagements, including projections and forecasts; conduct of internal firm inspection; and supervision of various audit engagements. Clients include nonprofit organizations, retail, wholesale distribution, manufacturing, construction, and state and federally assisted organizations.

1980 to 1993:
Madison Associates, P.A., CPAs (Chicago, IL)

Head Accountant

Audit engagements included publicly traded companies, consolidations of foreign subsidiaries, major construction companies, and federal and state funded nonprofit organizations. Tax preparation included individual and a variety of corporate situations.

1972 to 1980:
Brasse, Behrent, and Mark, CPAs (Madison, WI)

Supervisor

Oversaw design and implementation of firm's continuing education program. Performed firm's annual internal inspections. Audit engagements included domestic and foreign nonprofit organizations and a prominent overseas university. Performed operational and financial audits of both nonprofit and commercial organizations as well as liquidations, mergers, consolidations, spin-offs, business valuations, compilation and review engagements, and extensive corporate and individual income tax planning and preparation.

OTHER EXPERIENCE

Volunteer: WCXS (Rockwood, IL Public Radio affiliate). Phone campaign volunteer of **seventeen years standing;** currently help to schedule and coordinate group phone outreach campaigns once a month, and spend approximately six hours per month making telephone appeals.

Brantwell University
Waltham, MA

* Graduated 1972
* BS in Business Administration
* 3.4 Overall GPA
* 3.7 Accounting GPA

Downsizing is on the horizon! A senior executive with lots of experience in an upscale corporate environment appeals to a smaller, dynamic, firm—and downplays a relative lack of computer experience by highlighting other significant strengths.

Jane Smith
123 Main Street
Mytown, State 00000
111/000-0000

Strong Suits: Have a demonstrated record of **turning around cash-drain business areas a**nd selling off unprofitable operations. Well schooled in strategic planning, financial control, and business systems and procedures. Highly organized, detail oriented, and strongly analytical, with excellent written and verbal skills. Called **"a positive change agent."** Broad background in financial planning and control.

Work Highlights:

Americap, Glendale, CA (1994-present)
Vice President of Finance and Operations

Directly responsible for all general and cost accounting areas, monthly closings, financial analysis and reporting, budgeting, financial short- and long-term planning, business systems maintenance and new development. Oversee manufacturing and distribution, facility management, and interaction with corporate operations and executive management.

At Americap, I …

Helped troubled, cash-drain departments to become key contributors in at least six cases.
As part of Information Systems Users Committee, helped to **streamline reporting systems;** this resulted in more (and more accurate) reports from MIS department.
Launched restructuring program that improved company's cash position by **$35 million.**
Sold off three underperforming business units.
Improved companywide inventory management and fulfillment system; **reduced shipping delays by 26% and improved cash flow.**

Computer skills: Working proficiency in popular programs and environments.

Education: Verona (NJ) College, B.S. in Economics and Finance

STAFF ACCOUNTANT

The opening lines of the summary are highly targeted and thus help to put the odds in the applicant's favor. The inclusion of a job that helped to meet college financial obligations can be a real plus for the recent graduate. Don't be afraid to emphasize what you used the money *for* in this case.

John Smith
123 Main St.
Mytown, State 00000
111/000-0000

A skilled, energetic financial problem solver
highly qualified to make a contribution
as a Staff Accountant with ABC Corporation.

EDUCATION

University of Northern Connecticut
Bachelor of Science Degree, Accounting, May 1997
Accounting GPA: 3.45 (18 units)
Cumulative GPA: 3.58 (36 units)

Hartford Community College
Associate Degree, May 1994
Accounting GPA: 3.90 (16 units)
Cumulative GPA: 3.80 (62 units)

WORK EXPERIENCE

Tax Preparer
VITA (Volunteer Income Tax Assistance Program) 1993-1994
Hartford, CT

Helped senior citizens to complete income tax returns.
Developed familiarity with current tax requirements.
Utilized strong interpersonal skills to develop workable strategies for resolving tax questions.
Regional coordinator called my work "exemplary."

Assistant Manager
Frank's Place, July 1992 - December 1994
Hartford, CT

Accounted for daily cash balances.
Personally responsible for all inventory counts and reports.
Supervised crew of seven.
Trained and hired employees.
Planned and designed weekly menus.
My work at Frank's Place was part-time and helped to pay college tuition expenses.

Floor Supervisor
RyePack Co., January 1991 - July 1992

Tracked and managed daily and weekly schedules.
Supervised and evaluated employees.
Scheduled production activities and maintained quality control.
Used spreadsheet and data management software to prepare reports and analyses for top management.

I am skilled in using a wide variety of popular spreadsheet and data management software, including Microsoft Excel, Microsoft Access, and Lotus 1-2-3.

ACTIVITIES AND HONORS

University of Northern Connecticut Accounting Society - Member, Spring 1997
Interests - Baseball, basketball, soccer (played on intramural teams in all three sports).
Fluent in French and Spanish

Please call my references at your convenience!

Mel Vestro, Volunteer Income Tax Assistance Program, Hartford, CT (203/555-1213)
Frank MacDonald, Frank's Place, Hartford, CT (203/555-1214)

8

Resumes That Take Big Risks

Practical Tips When "Desperate Times Call for Desperate Measures"

Believe me, the secret of the greatest fruitfulness and the greatest enjoyment of existence is to live dangerously.
FRIEDRICH NIETZSCHE

You may not want to use the ideas in this chapter for every employment situation. But, for some opportunities, you may be justified in "tossing the dice" to see what happens next.

Another example of a dramatic effect that can be produced with relatively little fuss on a contemporary word processing program. Note how the omission of a date in the educational section eliminates the possibility of "lost years"—in this case, a possible area of concern due to an unfortunate mismatch on the writer's (unmentioned) first professional position.

Jane Smith
123 Main St.
Mytown, State 00000
111/000-0000

A GOAL-ORIENTED STAR PERFORMER FOR ABC CORPORATION

SUMMARY OF QUALIFICATIONS

★ Demonstrated ability to handle the increased challenges of a constantly changing, fast-paced work environment.

★ Attain proficiency in new applications quickly and easily.

★ Offer strong PC skills in all popular programs.

SELECTED ACCOMPLISHMENTS

★ Surpassed company targets in staff promotion and retention.

★ Overhauled spreadsheet operations, leading to increased staff productivity.

★ Developed systems that have resulted in "superior expense control" and "increasingly focused forecasting" (company newsletter, 1/97).

★ Initiated four new and successful employee training programs.

PROFESSIONAL EXPERIENCE

JJG, INC. • Berkeley, CA, 1993 - Present.
A $625 million firm specializing in retail marketing of children's clothing.

Accounting Manager

Direct responsibility for managing the Accounting Department of a $27 million division. Active in all aspects of budgeting and forecasting, preparation of financial statements, and inventory management. Interact and work closely with Marketing Department and Divisional Vice President. Supervise, motivate and train a staff of six entry-level accountants. Improved cash flow through recommendations for changes in refund payment methods.

BELLWORTH MANAGEMENT • Stamford, CT, 1986 - 1990
A Fortune 300 insurance brokerage firm.

Supervisor of Accounting and Office Services (1987 - 1990)

Earliest to be promoted to this title in company's history. Oversaw accounting and personnel tasks including maintenance of financial relationships with insurance carriers, preparation and presentation of annual budget, and supervision and direction of a staff of seven. Handled collection of aged accounts receivable and coordinated collections and payments to maximize holding period.

Accountant/Clerk (1984 - 1986)

Entry-level accounting department position. Handled accounts receivable entries, prepared daily deposits, maintained fixed asset records and related journal entries, and performed a wide variety of related accounting tasks.

EDUCATION

Starkey College, Mill Valley, CA

Bachelor of Arts • Business

Administration/Accounting

Aggressive? Informal? Maybe. Unprofessional? Naah. Here's a resume that's brave enough to acknowledge that it's an advertisement for solutions. It may not be a conservative manager's cup of tea, but then again, if the network's been down recently ...

John Smith
123 Main St.
Mytown, State 00000
111/000-0000

WHILE YOUR PC GENTLY WEEPS ...

... over long lag times and inaccurate forecasts, consider this. I am a seasoned contributor with a proven ability to deliver accurate results that help to improve your bottom line. My six years of experience have left me highly skilled in the operation of ...

* IBM-compatible workstations, local area networks, peripherals and utilities

* PC and network operating systems and tools (including Windows 95, Norton Utilities, etc.)

* Software packages such as MS Office (Word, Excel, PowerPoint, Mail) and Lotus SmartSuite, as well as many other popular programs. I am at ease in both PC and Macintosh environments.

Employment Experience

Data Technology Consultants
Financial Data Management Consultant
1994 - Present

Client: State of Illinois

* Designed and researched the first departmental Information Management Plan for the Department of Business Development of the State of Illinois.

* Coordinated the departmental process for preparing the annual Data Management Plan.

* Streamlined departmental information management and financial planning systems.

Glossman Corporation
General Manager
1992 - 1994

* Directed 75 technology consulting, sales and administrative staff producing $5,500,000 in revenue.

* Supervised establishment of client server network.

* Allocated resources for an in-house research, development and training facility.

Senior Administrator
1989 - 1994

* Established accounting, budgeting, chart of accounts, project costing, financial analysis, management reporting and profit sharing/bonus systems.

* Prepared, negotiated and administered successful multimillion-dollar project proposals.

* Helped establish local area network, integrating mission, objectives, and operational practices.

* Coordinated sales forecasting, recruiting, contract administration, asset management, bidding and human resource practices as part of 320% growth during first three years.

Education

* Belson University, Master's Degree in Public Administration, 1988

* Calipha College, Bachelor's Degree in Politics (Honors) 1985

STOP THE SOBBING! CONTACT ME AT THE ADDRESS ABOVE SO WE CAN DISCUSS
EFFECTIVE SYSTEM SOLUTIONS FOR ABC CORPORATION.

An impossible-to-ignore opening that projects both confidence and thorough, informed professionalism. Note the emphasis on the applicant's ability to shift between individual- and team-oriented work settings—an important asset in many of today's flattened organizations.

Jane Smith
123 Main St.
Mytown, State 00000
111/000-0000

My research of ABC Corporation leads me to believe that you are looking for someone with ...

... five years of experience as Accounting Manager, Auditor, and Business Systems Analyst. That's me! My specific areas of strength include:

accounting management

analysis

general ledger preparation

operations and compliance audits

PROFESSIONAL HISTORY

Freestone Credit Union (Freestone Technologies) - Sacramento, CA
11/92 - Present

Accounting Manager

Supervise seven accounting staff. Maintain general ledger, fixed asset depreciation schedule, and various income amortization schedules. Prepare journal vouchers for monthly accruals, income amortizations, and corrections. Prepare monthly financial and statistical reports, audit schedules, end of month closing entries, weekly reports, quarterly profit and loss statements, and quarterly employer's federal tax reporting. Prepare annual property tax rendition. **Assist with annual reports and meet with regulatory representatives.**

Business Systems Analyst

Provide work process analysis; system design; planning and acceptance testing of modifications to Freestone's FactAccess data delivery system. Develop internal documentation for information system program changes. Evaluate and install software; **develop computer training and support programs for users ranging from entry-level hires to senior management.**

Internal Auditor

Performed the planning and implementation of audits of 27 branch offices, 7 of which required travel, and 11 departments, to ensure compliance with state and federal regulations and Freestone guidelines. **Formulated audit conclusions and issued recommendations to management** concerning audit findings. Prepared formal written audit reports for management, board of directors, and audit committee. Assisted outside auditor's testwork.

Data Systems, Petaluma, CA
5/91 - 11/92

Financial Manager

Developed monthly financial and statistical reports, end of month closing entries, monthly profit and loss statements, monthly state sales tax reports, franchise tax reports, quarterly employer's federal tax reporting, payroll through ADP, and annual reports. Maintained general ledger, fixed asset depreciation schedules, and various amortization schedules. Interfaced with management, employees, State examiners, and external auditors. Developed information system for senior management by linking accounting system to spreadsheets via local area network. **Accurately forecasted cash flows based on sales and trends analysis.**

OTHER THINGS YOU SHOULD KNOW ABOUT JANE SMITH...

* Licensed Certified Public Accountant - State of California

* Highly skilled with numerous hardware and software applications including
   - Windows 95 and 3.x
   - Excel; Word; LAN-related applications

* Shift easily between a team environment and situations requiring individual contributions.

EDUCATION

Bachelor of Science in Business Administration / Accounting - December 1990

University of Pomona, Pomona, CA

Here's a resume that definitely puts the ball in the prospective employer's court! All the same, you should be prepared to follow up on your own via telephone.

Jane Smith
123 Main St.
Mytown, State 00000
111/000-0000

My references have kindly agreed to respond within 24 hours to any e-mail or phone queries concerning my candidacy. If you wish to reach them, here's how you can do so at any time:

Mel Brenson, Brentwood & Co. (brenson@brentwood.com) 510/555-1213 **"The sharpest, fastest, and most accurate auditor I've yet had the privilege to work with."**

Art Rodriguez, LightWays, Inc. (art@fastnet.com) 415/555-1212. **"A significant asset to our organization."**

Allison Darwell, Instructor, Crystal University (darwell@crystal.edu) 617/555-1212, **"A 'natural' who does what she loves and loves what she does."**

Experience

*   Auditor, 8/95 to present
Smith & Freehall, Boston, MA

Auditor: Clients include a major literary magazine publisher, a national homeowners association, various government-related projects through the Department of Health and Human Services, and real estate development and construction organizations.

*   Staff Accountant, 3/95 to 7/95
Brentwood & Co., Brookline, MA

Worked both in audit and tax areas. Highest number of billable hours in Brookline office. Assisted in audits of automobile dealerships, time share homeowners association and developer. Prepared tax returns for individuals and organizations of significant net worth.

*   Director of Billing, 11/89 to 8/94
Simpson & Associates, San Francisco, CA

Supervised staff of seven, insured that all legal bills were properly prepared, created and maintained 1-2-3 spreadsheets, instructed employees in the use of 1-2-3 spreadsheets and Wang and WordPerfect word processors.

* Director of Billing, 5/85 to 11/89
LightWays, Inc., Oakland, CA

Supervised staff of six, insured that all shipments were correctly invoiced, prepared summaries for general ledger, assisted Credit and Collections with reconciliations, prepared sales tax returns for several states, acted as backup personnel for Accounts Receivable and Accounts Payable, assisted Data Processing with backups and debugging.

Academics

* Master of Accountancy, Crystal University, May 1996; received Graduate School Honors, GPA 3.65 overall, 3.9 accounting.

* BBA - Accounting, BS - Computer Science, Carwell University, May 1995

Here's a resume that will *only* work in situations where you've identified a particularly striking match between what you know how to do and the nature of the work the employer needs done. Expect some fireworks when that match exists!

Jane Smith
123 Main St.
Mytown, State 00000
111/000-0000

SPECIFIC SKILLS FOR SPECIFIC PROBLEMS

A talented, creative, and experienced financial professional with practical strengths in the following critical areas of interest to ABC Corporation.

Government Contract Litigation

* Skilled in preparing claims involving U.S. Government contracts.

* Deep experience in assisting attorneys with cost accounting issues (and particularly adept at drafting questions for legal proceedings).

* Create and manage databases tracking all types of documents.

* Offer expert witness services. (I have appeared in 39 court proceedings as an expert witness on various topics.)

Forensic Accounting Services

* Offer reclamation and documention services for alleged embezzlements and fraudulent transactions.

* Skilled in the reconstruction of accounting records.

* Provide flow charting, graphic presentations, and expert witness services.

Pension/Profit Sharing/401(k) Plans

* Provide individuals and groups with compliance issues consultation.

* Plan audits.

* Counsel affected parties on preparing IRS Form 5500.

"They know enough who know how to learn." — Henry James

Another example of a high-profile guarantee, this one referenced at the beginning and end of the resume. It's a real showstopper.

Jane Smith
123 Main Street
Mytown, State 00000
111/000-0000

A GUARANTEED Fit in Finance Administration

AllSet Parking
San Francisco, CA (1995-present)

Currently supervise nine managers and eighty cashiers as the General Manager. I oversee 16 fee managed properties on a daily basis, develop annual budgets and track both revenue and expenses on a monthly basis. I have 3 years of experience with AllSet.

Meliss Engineering
Oakland, CA (1992-1995)

I worked in a variety of Cost Management and Internal Audit positions. I was selected as one of 13 candidates in Denver to participate in a 27-month rotational training program with Meliss. I have excellent computer skills and am well versed in both IBM and MacIntosh platforms.

I have an excellent working knowledge of Lotus 1-2-3, Microsoft Excel, Microsoft Word, Microsoft Access, Lotus 1-2-3, and MacDraw.

I performed audits on all major accounting systems at Meliss including Payroll, Accounts Payable, Revenue, Billing, Labor, Treasury and Purchasing.

Performance Highlights:

AllSet Parking:

Meet on a regular basis with various property managers and owners to discuss monthly financials, day-to-day operations, rate structures, staffing and other issues. **Operations costs have been reduced by 16% since I began at AllSet.**

Meliss Engineering:

Praised by senior partner during performance evaluation as **"the best thing to happen to the accounting department in a very long time."**

GUARANTEE:
I will commit to monthly self-reviews of my performance in your department and will submit concise written reports of progress toward mutually defined goals.

FINANCIAL RESEARCH ANALYST

An exceptionally strong guarantee, highly customized. Again, don't make promises like this one unless you can back up your talk!

Jane Smith
123 Main St.
Mytown, State 00000
111/000-0000

PROFILE: Extensive qualifications in research and research analysis. Superior analytical skills; cited for **"ability to identify and make intelligent recommendations about situations in which operative systems should be refined to contain costs and enhance revenue streams."** (Written excerpt from exit interview, July 13, 1997.)

MY GUARANTEE TO ABC:

Any employment offer is considered provisional upon the *overachievement, within 30 days,* of mutually determined written goals as a financial research analyst for ABC Corporation. *I will not accept a full-time offer of employment, probationary or otherwise, until this thirty-day overachievement condition has been satisfied.*

EDUCATION:

Ph.D., Finance, 1994, Whitewater Tech, Albany, GA

M.B.A., Finance, 1986, Pennsylvania Institute of Management, Philadelphia, PA

B.S., Finance, 1984, New York Institute of Technology, Buffalo, NY. Accorded highest honors.

HIGHLIGHTS:

Quantitative Research Analyst, Newton Financial Corporation, Atlanta, GA, 1996-present.

*   Conducted research using databases such as Compustat and Dow Jones News Retrieval. **Received "outstanding" rating in most recent personnel evaluation.**

Graduate Research Assistant, Department of Finance, Whitewater Tech., Albany, GA 1992-1994.

*   Assisted in the development of training materials that later served as the basis for my professor's textbook, *Fundamentals of Financial Research Analysis*. **Praised for "practical, profit-oriented approach" by Professor Warren Harrison.**

Intern, Accounting Today *magazine, New York, NY 1984.*

*   Helped in the evaluation of articles and filler pieces. Conducted telephone interviews and other support work for in-house editorial pieces. Described as **"one of the finest researchers ever to take part in the internship program"** by publisher Samuel Shanahan.

References:

Samuel Shanahan, Publisher, *Accounting Today* magazine (212/555-1213).

Warren Harrison, Professor, Finance Department, Whitewater Tech (404/555-1214).

SEEKING ENTRY-LEVEL POSITION

A highly targeted objective that incorporates a memorable guarantee. Specificity counts!

John Smith
123 Main St.
Mytown, State 00000
111/000-0000
Email:johnsmith@jjj.net

OBJECTIVE

To obtain an entry-level position in accounting or finance with ABC's Austin, Texas branch office.

EDUCATION

University of Texas at Austin; Bachelor of Science Degree,
December 1996
Major: Economics
Minor: Political Science

Served as Business Manager for Make a Joyous Noise (campus choir group, mounted three productions per year).

Volunteered at Weston Street Shelter, providing office support and general accounting help.

Received 100% score on final exam in Macroeconomics 101.

WORK EXPERIENCE

*　BILLING MANAGER/HTML PROGRAMMER
Paint Pro, Inc., Austin, TX, Summer 1996

I dramatically improved the billing system at Paint Pro, reducing bad debt by 15% and easing the load on the collections department. I also designed the firm's World Wide Web site (http://www.paintpro.com).

*　INTERN for U.S. Representative Melanie DiPresti, Summer 1995

I provided general office support and served as Campus Coordinator for various activities within Representative DiPresti's district. She later wrote that I "represent what is possible when youth, energy, commitment, and accountability intersect in a single individual."

OTHER HIGHLIGHTS

　*　Member of THETA SIGMA EPSILON - Economic Honor Society.
I headed the Community Outreach Committee.

　*　Strong software skills.
I am familiar with most popular spreadsheet, word processing, and data management programs.

　*　Speed reading graduate.
I read at approximately 500 words per minute, and have completed the Jane Powers Accelerated Reading Course.

> **GUARANTEE:**
>
> **If I accept an offer for an entry-level position with ABC Corporation and do not meet your expectations after 30 days, I will cheerfully submit my resignation.**

A highly targeted appeal that concludes with a bang. This aggressive, confident model could be adapted to any number of formats—but be prepared to back up your claims of a "perfect fit!"

Jane Smith
123 Main Street
Mytown, State 00000
111/000-0000

THE RIGHT INTERN FOR ABC COMPANY.

I recently completed my junior year as an Economics major at Mondale College. I am looking for a summer internship in the financial services or accounting areas. I possess a strong interest in the fields of financial services and banking.

WORK EXPERIENCE:

Bank of Anytown
Contact my former supervisor: Brenda Calli (111) 000-0000

During the summer of 1996, I worked as a bank proof operator for the Bank of Anytown, where my supervisor commented that she **"wish(ed) we had twenty more like you."**

My duties included:

Accurately processing transaction items from southern branches.

Endorsing and encoding checks, deposit tickets, charge-offs, wire transfers, currency transfers, and other similar items using 10-key bank proof item-processing machines.

I maintained a perfect attendance record during my tenure at Bank of Anytown.

Buell Center
Contact my supervisor: Fred Creech (111)-000-0000

During the college school year, I am a student research assistant at the Elizabeth Buell Policy Institute, a public policy think-tank in Normal, IL. My supervisor, Fred Creech, described me as **"a person born to deal with numbers."** He will be happy to provide you with a phone reference concerning my performance.

As part of my job, I...

Research and develop data via telephone interviews with low-income housing residents.

Assemble accurate totals for each of my calls.

Perform direct data entry onto the Institute's computer system in Microsoft Access.

Develop statistical reports based on my telephone work in Microsoft Excel.

Feldberg Library
Contact my former supervisor: Ellen Newberry (111)-000-0000

In past semesters, I have worked as a library assistant at the college's Feldberg Library. My duties have included...

Gathering and reshelving library material (requiring extensive knowledge of the library's shelving system).

Providing register assistance in book sales.

Performing data entry for library acquisitions.

I am fluent in French and Spanish.

I have extensive experience in the use of Microsoft Excel, Microsoft Access, Microsoft Word, WordPerfect Suite, Lexis/Nexis, and Netscape.

I've done a good deal of research on this opportunity; my conclusion is that we should work together.

A particularly powerful example of an end-of-resume guarantee. Don't make such a promise, however, unless you feel motivated to deliver on it!

John Smith
123 Main St.
Mytown, State 00000
111/000-0000

PROFILE

Seasoned **senior executive** named by *New England Business Journal* as **"One of the Fifty Most Effective Executives in Massachusetts"** (June 1993 issue).

Experienced financial professional with significant experience in **financial operations and corporate management.**

Personal responsibility for **P/L, strategic forecasting, and budgeting** functions.

PROFESSIONAL HIGHLIGHTS

Vice President of Finance and Operations, Westview Electric Company, Worcester, MA (2/94-9/98)

Responsible for overall business activity for this $22 million mechanical and electronic repair business. Increased new-customer base by **212 percent,** and annual income by over **100 percent.** Successfully implemented both internal and external benchmarking procedures.

Vice President of Finance and Operations, Daemon Corporation, Boston, MA (1/91-2/94)

Oversaw all financial and administrative operations for divisional headquarters of this $180 million consumer products firm. Supervised design and implementation of new Management Information Services system, resulting in dramatic **efficiency increases in data management and new product selection.** Reduced staff at division by **17 percent** without firing or laying off a single employee.

Operations Manager, Daemon Corporation (1/89-12/90)

Selected, designed, and oversaw implementation of data processing hardware and software. **Evaluated and revised order entry and inventory management systems, resulting in 21 percent improvement in average shipment time** and **14 percent reduction in inventory management time** by warehouse personnel.

Area Administrator, Daemon Corporation (1/88-1/89)

Handled a broad range of duties, including purchasing management and warehouse redesign. **Named "Manager of the Year" two years in a row.**

EDUCATION

University of Dallas, Dallas, TX
B.S. Degree in Accounting, 1987

I make a habit of putting my commitments in writing: If I accept your offer of employment and do not meet your expectations after the first 90 days on the job, ***I will voluntarily resign*** *and relinquish any claim to unemployment compensation funded by your firm.*

STAFF ACCOUNTANT

The guarantee in the Overview section is likely to make the prospective employer think twice before dismissing this applicant. What happens if the review isn't "excellent"? This applicant more or less leaves that up to the hiring official.

Jane Smith
123 Main Street
Mytown, State 00000
111/000-0000

Overview: **I guarantee** that I will receive an "excellent" evaluation from you on my first formal personnel review as a Staff Accountant.

Experience

The Choate Academy / Office Secretary
1996 to Present

Responsibilities include:

    Accurate preparation of monthly and quarterly accounting reports

    Providing support and appropriate input for end-of-year processing

    Monitoring attendance at Academy events and reporting results to appropriate offices

    Assist senior Academy personnel in evaluating financial data

    Preparing and updating Academy spreadsheets

    Responding to questions from students, teachers and visitors

Kennedy's / Cashier
1994 to 1996

Responsibilities included:

    Steadily greater accountability in cash handling and reporting functions (Eventually responsible for nightly bank deposits.)

    Customer service (Won Employee of the Month award six times.)

    Assisted in daily store operations; served as interim manager on several occasions.

Education

Accounting/Microcomputing Specialist Diploma, American Technical Institute, Wellfleet, MA

9

Don't Send It Off Yet!

Double-Check Everything

Chi Wen Tze always thought three times before acting. Twice would have been enough.

CONFUCIUS

No matter how excited you are about the opportunity you're pursuing, don't consider your resume and cover letter complete until you've consulted the following checklists!

There are plenty of resume horror stories making the rounds. I've heard of resume writers who committed grievous spelling errors in the very lines in which they boasted about their attention to detail; resume writers who focused on catastrophes at work that they vowed not to repeat; and resume writers who let ludicrously inappropriate word choices torpedo their chances for getting a good job. Don't let that happen to you! Follow the Ten Commandments for Perfect Cover Letters and Ten Commandments for Perfect Resumes.

Ten Commandments for Perfect Cover Letters

Thou Shalt Customize Thy Document to Thy Intended Audience.

Thou Shalt Focus Thy Remarks within a Few Concise Paragraphs, and Shalt in No Wise Exceed a Single Page.

Thou Shalt Read Thy Letter Carefully and, if Possible, Subject It to a Computerized Spell Check.

Thou Shalt Then, in Addition to Thy Computerized Spell Check, Enlist a Trusted, Literate Friend to Review Thy Text for Spelling or Style Errors.

Thou Shalt Never Bring Up Salary Unless Instructed by Thy Contact to Do So, in Which Case Thou Shalt Speak of Broadly Scaled Salary Ranges.

Thou Shalt Never Focus on a Negative Element of Thy Background.

Thou Shalt Use the Word "I" with Restraint.

Thou Shalt Include Full Contact Information in Thy Letter.

Thou Shalt Close Thy Letter with a Promise of, or a Request for, Future Action.

Thou Shalt Always Tell the Truth.

Ten Commandments for Perfect Resumes

Thou Shalt Customize Thy Document to Thy Intended Audience.

Thou Shalt Not Bore.

Thou Shalt Read Thy Resume Carefully and, if Possible, Subject It to a Computerized Spell Check.

Thou Shalt Then, in Addition to Thy Computerized Spell Check, Enlist a Trusted, Literate Friend to Review Thy Text for Spelling or Style Errors.

Thou Shalt Include Facts That Buttress Thy Cause, and Only Facts That Buttress Thy Cause, Never Confusing Thy Resume with a Confessional Document.

Thou Shalt Display Energy, Creativity, and Personality without Exceeding the Bounds of Good Taste and Professionalism.

Thou Shalt Break Thy Points Up into Readable Chunks.

Thou Shalt Eliminate Fluff and Trivia That Supports Not Thy Cause.

Thou Shalt Include Full Contact Information in Thy Resume.

Thou Shalt Always Tell the Truth.

Review these lists, check them twice, bear them in mind as you compose your written appeals—and your campaign to land the finance job you deserve will have been well and truly launched.

Good luck!

Index